REAL WORLD
TRAINING
DESIGN

**Navigating Common Constraints
for Exceptional Results**

Jenn Labin
Foreword by Ruth Colvin Clark

ASTD
PRESS

ASTD Press is an internationally renowned source of insightful and practical information on workplace learning and performance topics, including training basics, evaluation and return on investment, instructional systems development, e-learning, leadership, and career development. Visit us at www.astd.org/astdpress.

Ordering information: Books published by ASTD Press can be purchased by visiting ASTD's website at store.astd.org or by calling 800.628.2783 or 703.683.8100.

Library of Congress Control Number: 2011944559
ISBN-10: 1-56286-815-2
ISBN-13: 978-1-56286-815-4

ASTD Press Editorial Staff:
Director: Anthony Allen
Senior Manager, Production & Editorial: Glenn Saltzman
Community of Practice Manager, Learning & Development: Juana Llorens
Associate Editor: Ashley McDonald
Associate Editor: Heidi Smith
Associate Editor: Stephanie Castellano

Design and Production: Insoo Kim
Cover Design: Ana Foreman

Printed by Versa Press, Inc. East Peoria, IL, www.versapress.com

Contents

Foreword

All instructional projects have a back story. You learn the back story as your clients say things like:

"We really don't have time for any analysis–we need to get the product out there next month."

"Yes, it would be nice to have some practice exercises but we can't let the staff off the floor for more than 30 minutes at a time–just summarize the basics in a PowerPoint."

"I saw a keynote on games and social media so let's focus on those in this program!"

Real World Training Design is a streamlined guide to the ADDIE model of the instructional systems design (ISD) process. Rather than lengthy chapters on each phase (analysis, design, development, implementation, and evaluation) you get a road map with stops that offer guidelines and tools for the back story of your instructional journey.

You will find a guide to address the three main constraints that shape all training efforts: time, cost, and quality constraints. Yes, you will get a snapshot of the basic elements of each stage, but the main focus is on how to adapt ADDIE to those constraints of time, cost, and quality. As the author points out, you will probably never hear phrases like, *"Take all the time and money you want for this training project."*

I've seen articles and conference presentations that vilipend ISD with projections of its death or obsolescence. However, as training professionals our work risks irrelevance when we ignore a systematic process to align training to business goals. And the ADDIE model–or whatever variation you want to use–is a proven process to identify, align, promote, and sustain those bottom line objectives. At the other extreme, an obsessive adamantine approach to ADDIE can render results that are equally irrelevant as ignoring it altogether. Excessive time invested in analysis and dotting all of the i's more often than not ends in a product that is too late or too bloated to be useful. The work of a training professional is always a juggling act to balance the many variables endemic in each project.

If you are looking for a detailed tome on ISD, move on. *Real World Training Design* is short, smart, easy to read, with a focus on the back story of time, resources, and quality constraints that shape every ISD effort. Each chapter includes a real-world case example along with a job aid to help you apply the methods to your own projects. Use this book as a reality check, whether you have learned most of your ISD in an academic setting or in the trenches.

Ruth Colvin Clark
March 2012

Preface

This book began as a conversation. Specifically, it originated from the countless passionate discussions I have had with mentees, new instructional designers, and other colleagues on the topic of learning and development.

Over the course of a decade, I have been fortunate enough to work with many people new to this industry. Almost every one of them goes through a sort of "culture shock" as they try to cram their academic view of training into a real world project. I have spent so many hours comforting peers as they try to sort through a derailed project, unhappy customers, and ineffective training programs. The underlying issues usually track back to a difficulty anticipating time, cost, and quality constraints on a project. And it's not just new folks who get sidelined with these factors–seasoned practitioners often get surprised as well.

I found myself jotting down the same models on the back of napkins over and over again. I shared my project management or design templates repeatedly. The processes that I developed were passed around to help my peers save time and money on their projects. That's when I realized that I wanted to share these tools, tricks, and tips with a wider audience.

My goal for this book is to provide both new and experienced professionals in the learning and development industry practical tools to better navigate the real world. The style of this book is intended to be a visual guide with pages that you can dog-ear and refer to when in need. There is plenty of whitespace for your notes, and chapter exercises for you to try out the skills discussed on those pages. Just as important, updated content and submissions from readers will appear on the *Real World Training Design* website (www .terpassociates.com/rwtd/) so that you can continue to benefit from this book, as well as from your peers

Jenn Labin
March 2012

Acknowledgments

There are a lot of people to thank, worship, and praise for this book. Elaine, thank you for being the GPS on my professional journey, I am so grateful for your wisdom and friendship. Thank you to my contributors: Trish and Mary–visionaries for change and inspiring leaders, Vicki–brilliant! and so generous to help out a total stranger, Janne–a force in the classroom and a great teacher, Wendy and Jim–your passion for measuring impact shapes our industry, Jean– a L&D leading lady who took on the challenge without blinking an eye. To Nancy Duarte–thank you for allowing me to build on your amazing and ground-breaking work. Thanks also go to ASTD editors Justin, Kristin, and especially Juana for dealing with this first time author. My gratitude to Kelly and Kevin, two of my SMEs, and to everyone else in PD for putting up with me this year. Many thanks to Insoo, whose creativity is at the heart of this book. Thank you to my family for things too numerous to count. Finally, to Jon and Zoë– thank you for your unwavering support while I drifted from room to room with my laptop, waiting for inspiration to strike.

INTRODUCTION

Do the difficult things while they are easy and do the great things while they are small. A journey of a thousand miles must begin with a single step.

- Lao Tzu

Real World Constraints

I live near Washington, D.C. and on occasion I need to go into the city. In order to get to my destination, there are a lot of different routes I can take. Sometimes, I'm running late and I will take highways to save time. Other times, I might be showing some friends the Air and Space Museum, so I will take a route that winds around some other landmarks to add to their experience. There are still other events that I know will begin and end around rush hour so I will take the Metro to avoid stop-and-go traffic and using a lot of fuel.

The point is, despite the constraints we face each day, we figure out the best way to reach our destination. Designing training is very similar to taking a day trip. Sometimes you need to find the most direct path to the finish line, or you need to find ways to reduce the budget, and sometimes the training is so critical that you have to invest all of your effort into improving the quality of the experience or into being compliant with regulations. Time, cost, and quality constraints are the obstacles encountered by every training project.

The purpose of this book is to help you navigate through these road hazards to get safely to your destination.

The ADDIE Model

Pick up any book about the basics of training and development and you will see the ADDIE model. The ADDIE process is one of many models that inform the way we (training professionals) go about building, delivering, and evaluating training programs.

There are many training design models out there besides ADDIE. However, ADDIE is the one we are using throughout this book. If you are not a fan of the ADDIE model, the content in this book should be applicable to whichever model you choose to follow.

If you are a practitioner, you should know the ADDIE model. You should be able to apply the ADDIE model. **Most importantly, you should be able to adapt the ADDIE process and components to your own specific situation and project.**

That's right. The ADDIE model is an **academic** model. Think of ADDIE as directions that you have printed out before driving somewhere. Once you're on the road, you encounter a major detour and all of a sudden you aren't really sure what to do. This book is intended to be your GPS or navigation system to tell you where to turn when things get hairy.

In the real world, whether that's in government, the private sector, or anywhere else, the ADDIE model is rarely followed perfectly–with each step given its due diligence. However, reacting to the constraints of the real world does not have to return diminished results. Success comes from being aware of the choices to be made and purposefully excluding or including certain steps.

This book is all about helping you cope with unexpected detours–and adapting your route to get to your destination on time and on budget.

What Is ADDIE?

Step of the Process	Top 3 Things You Need to Know
ANALYSIS	1. Project planning–scope, timetables, cost estimates and deliverables 2. Audience analysis–relevant demographic information 3. Content analysis–performance to be addressed by training
DESIGN	1. Objectives: What do you want your learners to do? 2. Training outlines give an overview of how you will achieve goals 3. Content is organized and prepared
DEVELOPMENT	1. Materials are created as needed 2. e-learning/m-learning is created as needed 3. Content is continually vetted and quality checked
IMPLEMENTATION	1. The training event takes place 2. A Pilot should be done (by situation) 3. Adjustments should be expected
EVALUATION	1. Level 1–Expectations/Reactions are measured 2. Level 2–Learning objectives 3. Level 3–Behavior change measured on the job 4. Level 4–Business results are measured

Some Tools/ Methods	Some Common Pitfalls
Surveys Interviews Observations Focus groups Extant data	• Skipping this step • Miscommunication with stakeholders • Spending time and money on methods that do not return impactful information
ABCD objectives Basic/detailed outlines Collaboration with SMEs	• Starting with this step • Spending too much time on plans and outlines • Not spending enough time aligning design to business
Workbooks Job Aids Wikis/Knowledge management Web design Collaboration with developers	• Underestimating the cost of development • Involving people too late • Not enough emphasis on user experience
Web conferencing software Collaboration with facilitators	• Not utilizing skilled facilitators • Not inviting stakeholders to participate • Spending too much money on details that don't impact learning
Surveys Interviews Data analysis	• Waiting until after a training event to begin this step • Spending effort measuring the wrong things

Time, Cost, Quality

Any given project in the real world is under siege by at least one of the three project management constraints. These constraints of time, cost, and quality/scope are the reason that purely academic approaches to projects will not work. Each constraint exerts certain pressures on a training design.

These constraints are typically represented as a triangle. Like the sides of a triangle, adjusting one constraint affects the others. A tight budget for a training project could mean increased time or smaller scope. A short deadline could mean that you will need to acquire more resources to get the project done and increase cost.

Ancient L&D Saying:

"You can have this training fast, cheap, or good. Pick two."

This book helps you to make effective choices within each constraint. Many of the "non-negotiables" in this book can be applied to multiple constraints. For example—creating "version controls" around documents is critical for short timelines, but also helps with cost and quality in the long run.

So, what if you are asked to create compliance training for a recent policy change—and you are given all of two weeks before you have to pilot it? What's the bottom line? Which steps are required and which can you skip? What shortcuts will mean an on-time deliverable and which will mean ineffective training?

How to Use This Book

This book is intended to help you overcome time, cost, and quality constraints as you complete a training project. You can start at the beginning and read each chapter, or, you can target the topics that are important to you right now.

Each chapter of the book is broken down as follows:

Overview: Introduction to the chapter

 By the Book: Basic definitions and information

 Speed Limits: Time constraints

 Toll Lanes: Cost constraints

 Scenic Route: Quality/Scope constraints

 Tour Guide: Case studies and real-life examples

 Fuel Up: Tools and templates to get you started

You're Just Getting Started

Being a learning and development (L&D) professional in today's world is fun, difficult, rewarding, complex, thankless, and exciting. Training is becoming increasingly effective, and infinitely less defined. Options for individuals to gain new skills and knowledge are expanding. Yet, our mission to help our workforce grow and develop has not fundamentally changed.

You may have gone to school to teach adults, or you may have lucked into it through some twist of professional fate. You may have taken a class, or workshop, or read a book to learn about instructional design. You may have never thought about designing training a minute in your life until your manager gave you this task.

You might have already learned about how very different the real world of training design is from the academic ideals in textbooks and whitepapers.

No matter what your journey has been, the intention of this book is to provide you with all of the tools, tips, and tricks you need to be successful on your trip.

You have a project in front of you, and (hopefully), stakeholder support behind you. The road ahead could be long or short, you could be on a scenic route or on the expressway…just be sure to bring this travel guide with you.

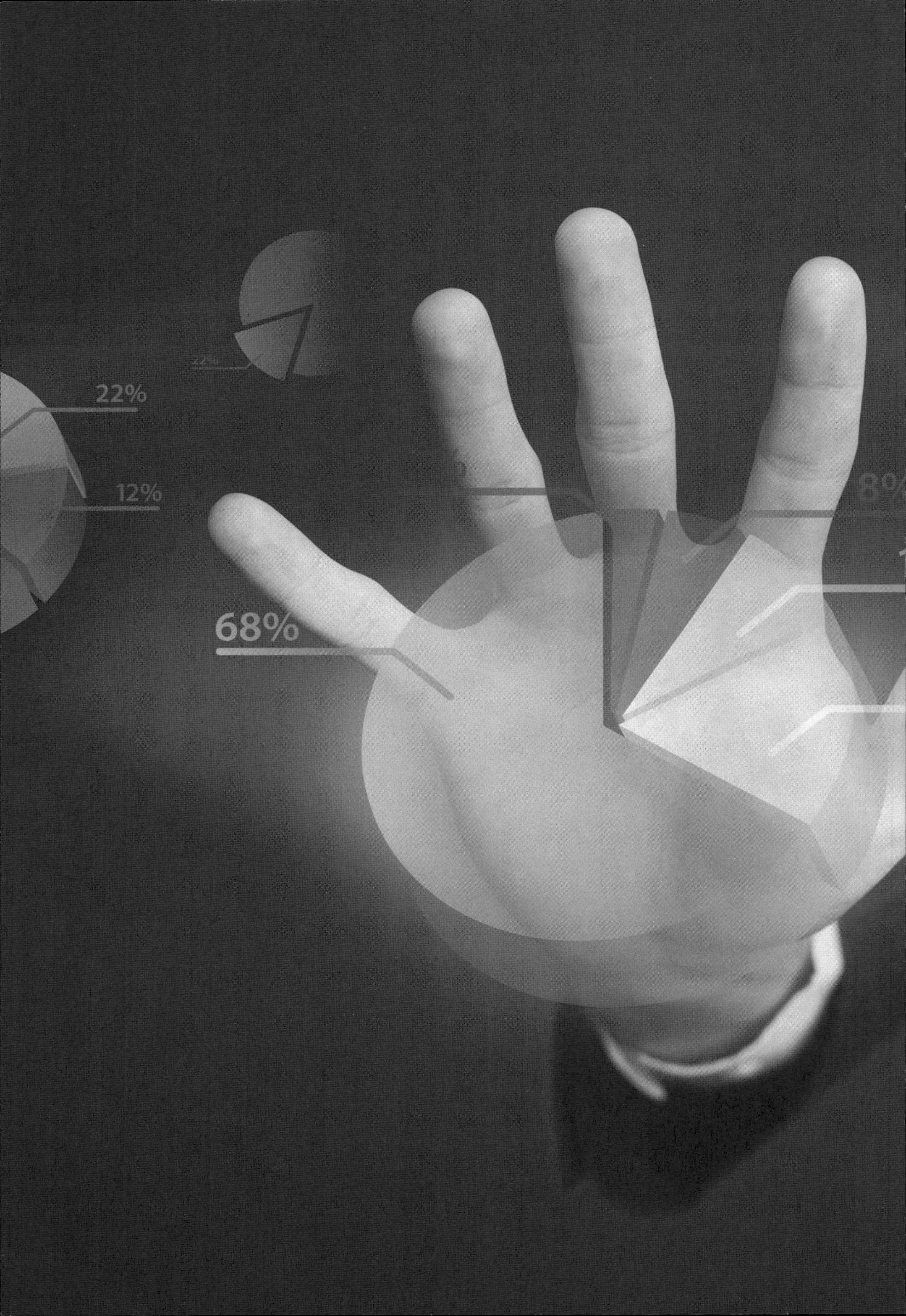
22%
12%
68%
8%

ANALYSIS

22%

Data is what distinguishes the dilettante from the artist.

- George V. Higgins

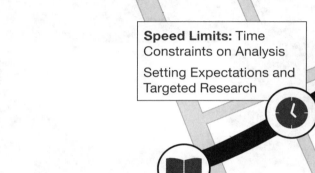

Speed Limits: Time Constraints on Analysis

Setting Expectations and Targeted Research

By the Book: Basic Definitions and Information About Analysis

ROAD MAP: What to Expect

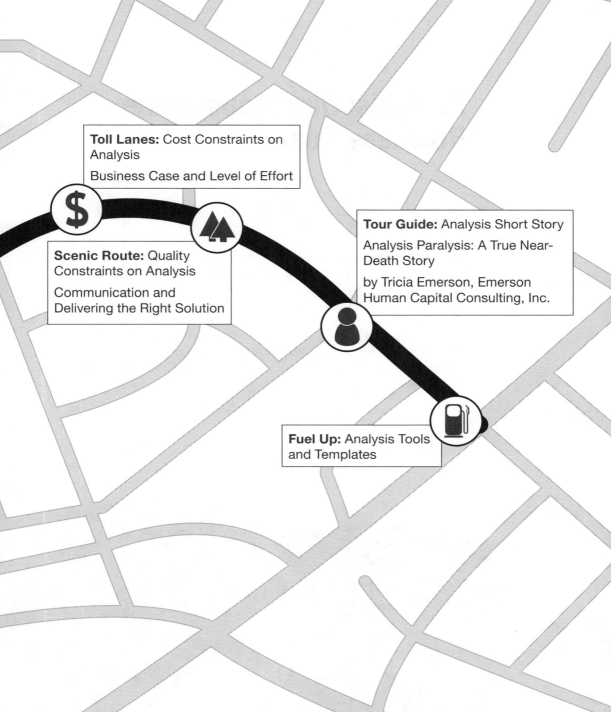

Toll Lanes: Cost Constraints on Analysis

Business Case and Level of Effort

Scenic Route: Quality Constraints on Analysis

Communication and Delivering the Right Solution

Tour Guide: Analysis Short Story

Analysis Paralysis: A True Near-Death Story

by Tricia Emerson, Emerson Human Capital Consulting, Inc.

Fuel Up: Analysis Tools and Templates

Analysis: Directions to the Business Goal

If your training project is a road trip, the analysis stage is when you pick your destination, find out what the weather will be like, and figure out local tourist spots. This is the first step in the ADDIE model of instructional systems design (ISD).

During analysis you focus on data gathering and examination. This stage involves identifying key characteristics of your audience and content to eventually create a clear path from your training event to performance change.

Bad directions on a vacation can have you heading toward Portland, Maine instead of Portland, Oregon. Similarly, skipping this step, like so many training projects do, could mean missing the training goal completely.

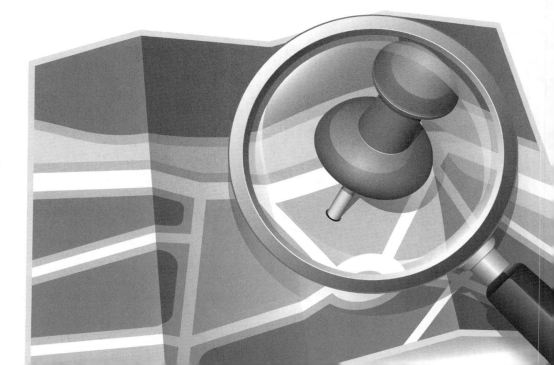

By the Book: Analysis

Traditionally, analysis implies a period of time devoted to assembling as much data regarding the training content and audience as possible. Then, those data are, sifted, sorted, chunked, prioritized, reviewed, and analyzed. This step is also called "front-end analysis," because these steps are done at the beginning of the project as opposed to throughout the process.

The purpose of analysis is to gather information in order to answer some fundamental questions about your project:

Key Questions:
- What business goal do you want to achieve?
- What is the performance/behavior/change required to meet that goal?
- What are the systemic factors (environment, supervision, technology, etc.) that contribute to the performance?
- Who will be affected by this performance/behavior/change?
- What will I see as a result of this training event that demonstrates the learning has occurred?

In a full-length, top-to-bottom, give-it-all-you-got analysis, data are collected on the job of the target audience. Then, the tasks and functions of that job are studied along with the performance measures of those tasks. The designer then compares the training need with existing developmental opportunities. If no current solution exists, information is gathered about the instructional needs of the audience.

Analysis Methodologies

Several methodologies are traditionally used to provide information during the analysis phase.

- **Observation:** Watch and document as someone performs the job/task.
- **Interview:** Ask pre-set questions of a representative group of people (individual contributors, supervisors, SMEs, customers).
- **Data Analysis:** Review documents, metrics, performance evaluations, organizational reports, and other information.
- **Focus Groups:** Formal and documented group discussions about the job/task.
- **Surveys:** Distribute questionnaires (digital or paper).

After the information is gathered, the designer compiles results into a useable format as an input for the next phase of the ADDIE model: design.

Project Management: The Map

Also during this phase, if not before, the project manager will complete some of the management deliverables such as timelines, milestones, and communication plans. These documents function as the road map for your training project. More accurately, a project plan is a navigation system with live and updated traffic information.

Can you get to the end of your journey without a map or GPS? Sure, but the trip becomes a lot easier if you have the ability to avoid traffic and construction at your fingertips.

For more on project management:

Check out *Project Management for Trainers* by Lou Russell (ASTD Press), a fantastic tool-based book on the subject.

🕐 Speed Limits: Time Constraints

If training projects had taglines, half of them would be, "We're on a short time table." Tight deadlines and pressures from internal and external clients are constant in the modern world of immediate need and immediate access. The unfortunate side effect of a shortened project cycle is often an ineffective half-hearted effort, or skipping this phase altogether. Luckily, it is possible to gather compelling data without sending your project timeline into a tailspin.

1. Set Appropriate Expectations–This is key, both with the people funding the training, and with your end users. You will prevent hours of re-work, and save your credibility, if you plan the project well and establish agreement on the goals of the training.

   a. Hold Kick-Off Meetings

   b. Create a Project Plan

2. Targeted Research–Avoid the typical scatter-shot method of analysis and focus on very specific information.

   a. Allow for Audience Assumptions

   b. Ask Bull's-eye Questions

   c. Perform the Sniff Test

Set Appropriate Expectations—Kick-Off Meetings

Always hold a kick-off meeting with your project's clients. Make sure that decision makers are in the room as the group determines the project's goals, scope, timelines, resources, and expected hurdles. Neglecting this step will almost guarantee setbacks later in the project.

KICK-OFF MEETING AGENDA

1. **Introductions:** Stakeholders, designers, facilitators, and SMEs introduce themselves and their role on the project. The project background and context are set by executive sponsor.

2. **Goals:** The importance of the project to the organization should be clearly stated for everyone to hear. The business goals of the project are outlined. These tend to fit under IR/AC/IS (increase revenue, avoid cost, increase service), but can also include goals such as increase employee engagement or retention, lower workplace accidents, increase compliance, and so forth.

3. **Scope/Milestones:** This is where the group will answer, "What does good look like?" What components will this training program have that will make it successful? Avoid getting into too much detail like specific learning activities. What are the specific milestones that will indicate success along the way?

4. **Timeline:** Clearly outline the expected timeline for the project Get buy-in on this step from the executive sponsor and all stakeholders.

5. **Budget:** This could be dollar amounts or general expected expenditures depending on your organization.

6. **Resources:** Besides the people in the room, identify who should be included at points during this project, including learners during analysis, supervisors during reinforcement, marketing during communication, and so forth.

7. **Communication:** How often, and using what methods, will you communicate internally with your stakeholders and externally with the audience? Be clear with expectations.

8. **Logistics:** What deliverables are expected? How will they be stored? Who has access to information? What policies and procedures need to be considered?

9. **Summary:** Agree on the next steps and who is responsible for them. Schedule reoccurring meetings. Send out meeting minutes.

Set Appropriate Expectations—Project Plans

I remember when my fifth grade English teacher had us "brainstorm" our upcoming essays. What a pain! I just knew that I could write the whole paper in less time than it would take to follow her steps. And yet, it turned out that the classmates who listened to the teacher always had fewer mistakes in their papers.

Project plans (in whichever form you choose) can seem daunting, overly complicated, or even useless if you haven't had to create one. However, project plans are the "brainstorms" of the adult learning world. Without even a basic project plan, your team and stakeholders will have a more difficult time collaborating with you. You may fail to prioritize or budget your time appropriately. You may even end up spending more time backtracking and making up for mistakes.

Stage	Start	Due	Resources	Deliverable
Intro	16-Mar	23-Mar		
Schedule Intro Meetings		18-Mar	JL	
Kick-Off w/ Stakeholders		23-Mar	JL, KS	✔
Analysis	24-Mar	24-Apr		
Create analysis plan		27-Mar	SM, JL	✔
Develope analysis		31-Mar	JL	
Send out survey		1-Apr	KS	
Conduct focus groups		7-Apr	SM	
Analyze data		20-Apr	SM, JL	
Present findings		24-Apr	JL	✔
Design	25-Apr	15-May		
Determine objectives		26-Apr	JL	✔
Create evaluation plan		27-Apr	JL	
Storymap		29-Apr	SM	✔
General training evaluation		2-May	KS	✔
Detailed outline		15-May	KS	

Targeted Research—Audience Assumptions

How do you save time with an audience analysis? Don't do one.

This may seem like unorthodox advice, but there are cases when skipping the audience analysis makes sense. For one thing, if you are an internal training professional, and you have worked with the same audience many times before, you probably have a good sense of what inspires the group and what triggers the group may be sensitive to.

In other projects, you might be tempted to figure out what learning styles you need to take into consideration with a certain group. Let me save you time—you need to consider *all of them*. The effectiveness of training is not about learning styles or preferences.

For more on learning styles and impact on the design process, see page 67.

What about generational preferences in learning? You have probably read and heard all about our challenges with the generations in the workplace today. There is certainly some complex and meaty information to be gained from investigating this. However, when time is of the essence, some assumptions can be made:

- All generations want to be included, engaged, inspired, and interactive.
- All age groups want training that is relevant to their life and job.
- All people want to be respected as adults with their own unique experiences and backgrounds.
- While younger groups tend to be more comfortable with some modes of technology (a simplification, I know), all people, regardless of age, want the use of technology to be easy, intuitive, and seamless.

There, we just shaved a couple of weeks off of your timeline!

Targeted Research—Bull's-eye Questions

A significant percentage of analysis tools floating around in the world suffer from a major problem. Many of the questions and formats resemble a fishing expedition rather than target practice. Compare the weak questions on the left with the more targeted bull's-eye questions on the right

Please list your age.	▶	On a scale of 1-5, how comfortable are you with Microsoft Word?
What is the most challenging aspect of your job?	▶	Do you feel that team politics hinder productivity in the department?
What training classes would you be interested in?	▶	Which of the following training classes would have an impact on your current role?
Are you comfortable selling product XYZ to customers?	▶	Are you able to articulate our value proposition for product XYZ to customers?
How many hours a week do you spend in meetings?	▶	How much time do you spend in meetings each week where you contribute value?

23

Targeted Research—The Sniff Test

Never ask your audience or stakeholders to provide answers that will end up in a digital wasteland. Focus *only* on the content, audience, or business attributes that you need to know for this training project. It is common to ask biographical data on surveys. If you do not have a clear and present need for this information, don't ask for it.

Perform the "**sniff test**" on your questions.

1. Schedule some time with a volunteer from your analysis group.

2. Ask the volunteer each of your questions and have the volunteer provide as many different realistic answers as he or she can think of.

3. For each response, ask yourself, "What does this mean to my project? Will I be able to use these answers in my design?"

4. If it doesn't "smell" useful–don't ask the question during your analysis!

What obstacles prevent you from providing stellar customer service?	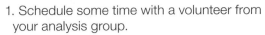	None–I have great satisfaction numbers. These old computers hold me back. Definitely! Everything! The processes here don't make any sense! There's too much paperwork just to help one customer.

In this example, the answers provided show great information from a systems standpoint, but they may not be much help to a specific training project. Edit and try again! Try the following targeted questions to replace our example:

- What knowledge or skills would help you provide better customer service? (Provide a list.)

- What issues have come up during your customer encounters that you would like more training on?

$ Toll Lanes: Cost Constraints

Tight budgets tend to go hand-in-hand with training. As with short timelines, cost cutting often leads to ineffective analysis. There are ways to save on money without sacrificing the entire analysis process.

1. Business Case—The ability to conduct an analysis will often come down to your ability to sell the value of gathering that data.

    a. Alignment of Analysis and Business Goals

2. Level of Effort—The tools and methods of analysis don't usually end up padding the budget; it's the billable hours that add up!

    a. Analysis Methods by Cost

    b. Virtual Focus Groups

Business Case—Alignment of Analysis and Business Goals

The analysis step tends to get shortcut or skipped because of our inability to make our business case. Simply put, one of the most important parts of any training designer's job is to be a good business partner–and that means showing the business case of analysis.

Always align your entire project under business goals. Don't even begin to think about conducting an analysis or starting a new project unless you know the results that your stakeholders want to see.

Make sure you can answer each of the following questions:

Analysis Question	Analysis Output – Business Case
What business goals are we trying to achieve with this project?	Business Goal
What on-the-job performance or behavior has to change in order to meet the business goals?	Performance Change
What learning needs to occur in order to affect the performance change needed?	Learning Goals
What are the characteristics of the audience that will affect learning?	Audience Data

Level of Effort—Analysis Methods by Cost

Most training projects use surveys if they conduct any analysis at all. Surveys are (generally) the fastest and cheapest method for gathering targeted information about your audience and performance needs. The following chart shows the relative cost for each analysis method. Notice that the cost is inversely related to the potential quality and detail of the data retrieved.

Observations:	Logistics can be complex Conduct individual sessions Compile varied data Analyze complex data
Focus Group:	Logistics can be complex Involves interpretation Compile varied data Analyze complex data
Interviews:	Conduct individual sessions Involves interpretation Analyze complex data
Extant Data:	Depends on others gathering info Compile varied data Analyze complex data
Surveys:	Depends on individual commiting to complete

Higher Quality of Data Gathered

Higher Cost (in work-hours)

Level of Effort—Virtual Focus Groups

Focus groups can yield a large amount of high-quality data. The benefit to using a cross-section of people to conduct your analysis is that you get many perspectives on the same topic at once–in addition, more time can be used to dive in deeper on certain answers to truly understand the context.

Focus groups can be costly, however. One way to avoid some of the cost and logistical issues is to set up a virtual focus group using your organization's virtual meeting software.

Schedule several 60- or 90-minute meetings– this gives group members time between meetings to think about additional points they would like to contribute.

Send questions to group members ahead of the meeting, allowing individuals to prepare for valuable conversation.

Establish rules for virtual discussion (for example each person is given a chance to respond to each question, and so forth).

Use meeting software to display flowcharts and relevant documents for feedback. Enable writing features to encourage participation.

After each session, summarize notes and send a copy to each member. Encourage them to respond with additional thoughts.

⛰ Scenic Route: Quality or Scope Constraints

The analysis stage is critical to making sure you are providing the highest quality training product, and helps to narrow project scope.

1. Communication–Establish expectations and status updates early for your project.

    a. Stakeholder Meetings

2. Deliver the Right Solution–Ultimately, the success of your training project comes down to solving a performance problem.

    a. Identifying Non-Training Issues

Communication—Stakeholder Meetings

Throughout the analysis phase—and the rest of the project—be sure to schedule frequent and consistent meetings with your stakeholders. Meeting regularly with the people who are important to the success of your project is the only insurance policy you have against road hazards.

 Ask your stakeholders what they would like to get out of each meeting. Once you figure out their expectations, make sure you deliver on them! Remember to speak strategically—stay away from "learning language" like "ADDIE" unless asked.

 If there is an important decision to make, having time set aside with your stakeholders can make your job easier. Before each meeting, send out an agenda and list any major decisions to be discussed.

 Regular meetings provide a chance to inform your stakeholders of unexpected problems that might come up. Remember, bad news early can be dealt with, bad news after the fact is too late!

 Don't forget to keep your stakeholders informed about good progress as well as challenges. Bring deliverables with you to meetings and provide visual milestones whenever possible.

 Use regular stakeholder meetings to ensure alignment with business goals and initiatives. The primary purpose of your meeting time is to stay on the right path, reduce re-work and keep informed of organizational needs.

Deliver the Right Solution—Non-Training Issues

The analysis phase of a project is when you can be a truly consultative business partner. Before plans are made for a specific type of class, with a certain kind of activity, you gather information about the reason for the project.

Be aware that not all performance issues can be solved with training. As a matter of fact, training is only the cure for very few illnesses.

If they **do not understand how** well they should complete the task, there is an issue with expectations. Consider resources for their managers instead.

If completing **the task is not rewarded,** or if skipping the task does not come with consequences, it could be an incentives issue.

If they don't know **how to do** the task, it is definitely a learning issue. However, training is not the only option.

If they **don't even know** that the task needs to be done, it might be a communications or management issue.

If they **don't believe in or understand** why they should do the task, it's a change management issue.

If people **do not have the support** needed to complete the task, it might be a time, money, or people resources issue.

👤 Tour Guide: Analysis Paralysis: A True Near-Death Story

Tricia Emerson, President and CEO, Emerson Human Capital Consulting, Inc.

Back in the 1980s, the Illinois Department of Employment Security (IDES) wanted a new training curriculum, and the analysis phase entailed a detailed review of their existing materials. The materials turned out to be thousands of binders and books, wedged into a windowless room on the 17th floor and covered in dust and mouse droppings.

This couldn't be the best use of my time, or their money. Was there no curriculum map for the existing programs? A set of objectives linked to courses? Or maybe an instructional design lead who could distill the learning approach during an interview? Apparently not. My client had directed me to review each of these musty tomes and report back. I was going to die in this place.

The binder room also included a 10-inch television airing daytime soaps for the enjoyment of Venus, the woman supervising the staff who provided janitorial services.

One day as I pored over a mountain of paper, I heard Venus's voice over the soap opera dialogue. She was talking on the phone, and the conversation went something like this:

"It's on fire? Is it still on fire? Go check and call me back."

Alarmed, I tried not to look like I was eavesdropping when the phone rang again.

"A supervisor? OK. Let me know what happens."

Back to the soaps. The phone rang again.

"What floor? Hmm, OK." Click. After 10 long minutes, another ring.

"I'm glad you took care of it."

Sensing a near-death experience, I had to pry. "Venus, what on earth is going on?"

"Well, someone in the 22nd floor cafeteria tossed a cigarette in the trash can and started a fire. My girl watched as the staff consulted procedures. They were required to call a supervisor, but they couldn't reach anyone on the phone. They sent a staff member, but the supervisor was on another level and the staff guy had to change elevator banks on the way. It was taking a long time. So my girl took the fire extinguisher from the wall behind the trash can and put the fire out herself."

The staff had resolutely followed the procedure and nearly burnt the place down. The process seemed logical, but the cleaning lady's gut told her there was a better way, and she took it upon herself to solve the problem.

Suddenly, I wanted to be that cleaning lady.

I needed to outsmart this analysis process. The project goal, the intent behind the project, became the guide for analyzing it. What clues might indicate instructional soundness? Maybe I could use that to quickly assess what courses might be useable. Armed with a checklist, I flew through the binders, culling the good from the bad. I delivered the analysis well under time and budget.

I was learning to use my head and trust my gut. My clients were overwhelmed, desperate for guidance, and that's why they'd hired me to do the analysis. I decided to deliver what they needed, not what I was asked for. Starting with that project, putting out fires became my specialty.

The tool I used to rapidly assess the instructional soundness of 10 million dropping-covered binders:

Clues to Instructional Soundness	Yes	No	N/A
1. Do the course objectives describe the behaviors a student should demonstrate?	☐	☐	☐
2. Does the content support the objectives?	☐	☐	☐
3. If there is a pre- or post-test, do the test items reflect the level of objectives?	☐	☐	☐
4. Is the instruction well organized?	☐	☐	☐
5. Are there opportunities to practice each major concept?	☐	☐	☐
6. Do participants practice the skills, as they will be applied on the job?	☐	☐	☐
7. Is the instruction interactive?	☐	☐	☐
8. Are the instructional strategies appropriate to the audience?	☐	☐	☐
9. Does the course emphasize the content's value to the participant (WIIFM)?	☐	☐	☐
10. Are new terms clearly explained?	☐	☐	☐
11. Does the content draw on the learner's past experience?	☐	☐	☐
12. Are there strong examples?	☐	☐	☐
13. Are there negative examples for difficult concepts?	☐	☐	☐
14. Are there summaries and reviews?	☐	☐	☐

Observations/Comments:

⛽ Fuel Up: Chapter Exercise

ALIGN PROJECT GOALS WITH BUSINESS GOALS

Answer These Questions:

1. What business goal do you want to achieve?

2. What is the behavior or performance change required to meet that goal?

Meet With Your Stakeholders:

3. Do they agree with your assessment of the goal of the class?

4. What additional feedback do they have?

CONDUCT AUDIENCE AND CONTENT ANALYSIS

Follow-Up Work:

5. What are the systemic factors (environment, technology, etc.)?

6. Who will be affected by this change?

7. What will I see as a result of this training event that demonstrates the learning has occurred?

⛽ **Fuel Up: Chapter Tool**

This is a "short but sweet" survey focused on gathering the training needs of any team of workers in an organization. This survey would be implemented after a communication issue was already known for the team. The results of this survey would clearly indicate what sort of communication training intervention would help this team.

For each of the following statements, indicate to what degree you agree or disagree on a scale of 1 (strongly disagree) to 5 (Strongly agree).

1. My direct supervisor sets clear expectations for my work.

2. My direct supervisor provides timely and helpful feedback on my work.

3. My direct supervisor tends to over-manage me (frequently checks over my work, gives direction on every task, does not allow for autonomy or creativity in approach).

4. My direct supervisor tends to under-manage me (rarely checks my work, does not give enough direction on tasks, expects creative solutions even on tasks I am not familiar with).

5. When I ask my peers for help, they are responsive and friendly.

6. When my peers ask for help, I understand what is needed and provide help as soon as I can.

7. There are individuals on my team who are overly-aggressive or disrespectful toward me.

8. There are individuals on my team who are shy and resigned–to the detriment of getting our work done.

9. There are individuals on my team who are social and talkative–to the detriment of getting our work done.

10. Meetings take the right amount of time to accomplish goals.

11. I feel comfortable with the conversations that I overhear from my peers and supervisor.

12. I am included in an appropriate amount of social, or non-work, conversations.

13. When my team or supervisor agrees to a task or an objective, I believe they will accomplish it.

14. I am comfortable approaching each of my teammates regarding concerns about my tasks and projects.

DESIGN

The mind has exactly the same power as the hands; not merely to grasp the world, but to change it.

- Colin Wilson

By the Book: Basic
Definitions and
Information About Design

ROAD MAP: What to Expect

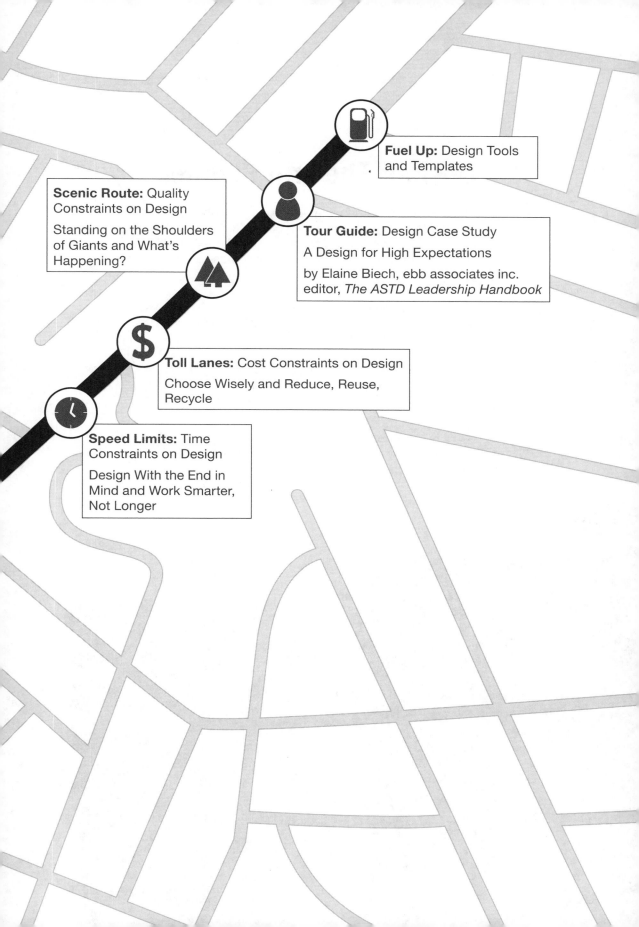

Fuel Up: Design Tools and Templates

Scenic Route: Quality Constraints on Design

Standing on the Shoulders of Giants and What's Happening?

Tour Guide: Design Case Study

A Design for High Expectations

by Elaine Biech, ebb associates inc. editor, *The ASTD Leadership Handbook*

Toll Lanes: Cost Constraints on Design

Choose Wisely and Reduce, Reuse, Recycle

Speed Limits: Time Constraints on Design

Design With the End in Mind and Work Smarter, Not Longer

Design: The Trip Planner

On our training road trip, the design stage is when we figure out our schedule and logistics, gather up our packing list, and figure out where to eat and sleep. By the end of this step, you know how your training intervention will solve performance issues and accomplish your business goals.

During the design phase, the data gathered during analysis are put to use to define what the training will look like, who should take it, when they should take it, and how you will know the training is successful.

Outputs of this design phase are learning objectives, performance measures, learning outline, and a learner profile.

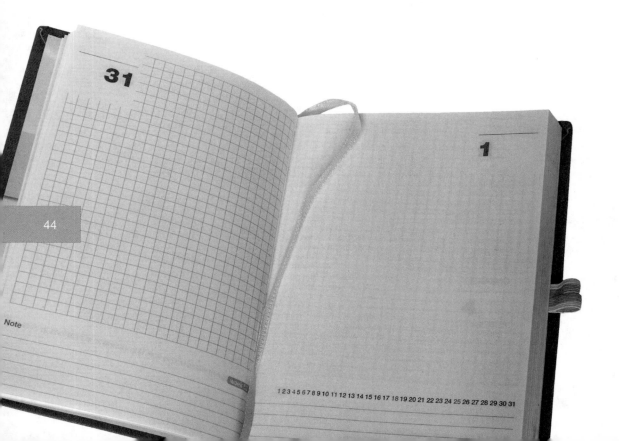

📖 By the Book: Design

During the design phase of the ADDIE process, designers develop learning objectives and a training outline—essentially the itinerary for the project.

The purpose is to put together the structure of the training in a manner that allows everyone on the project a clear view into key components based on the information gained from your analysis.

In the design phase, you will identify the objectives of the training, which will correspond to the business results defined previously. You will also indicate which performance metrics will help measure the behavior changes and create a training outline and facilitation points to correspond with your analysis results.

Design Step Breakdown

The "design" and "development" steps of the ADDIE model are often confused and jumbled together. While rapid ISD techniques combine these two steps (more on that later), it is still important to remember the key aspects of the design process.

Analysis Output	Design Considerations	Design Output
Business Goal	Alignment w/ business goals Provide strategic value	Learner-Centered Objectives
Training Outcomes	Behavior change as a result of training	Performance Measures (Evaluation Plan)
Learning Support	Specific skills and knowledge content to change behavior	Training Outline
Learner Profile	Learner characteristics such as motivators, obstacles	Facilitation Points/ WIIFM

We will address each design output throughout the remainder of this chapter.

⏱ Speed Limits: Time Constraints

The design step is at the heart of the ISD process. Taking the time to think up an effective and engaging training solution is the art within the science of L&D. However, there are several things you can do to save time during this step.

1. Design With the End in Mind–Plan your evaluation along with your design, not only will you save time, but your training will be more effective!

    a. Evaluation Planning

    b. ABCD Objectives

    c. Levels of Application

2. Work Smarter, Not Longer–Use smart collaboration techniques during the design phase to cut down the time waiting for others. Using "track changes," version control methods, and naming conventions will help keep your project on track.

    a. Version Controls and Naming Conventions

Design With the End in Mind—Evaluation Planning

Match your evaluation methods to your analysis results.

1. Organize analysis results into four deliverables.

| Business Goal | Increase revenue by 20% with the release of Widget Xtra. |

| Training Outcomes | Account representatives will upgrade 5,000 current customers to Widget Xtra and gain 3,000 new customers between November 2-13. |

| Learning Support | Reps will need to define the functions that differentiate the Widget Xtra, and identify customer account opportunities for upgrades. |

| Learner Profile | Reps are commission-based, with a bonus for top five in sales; geographically scattered; average tenure three years. |

2. Correspond to four levels of evaluation. How do we know if we hit those goals?

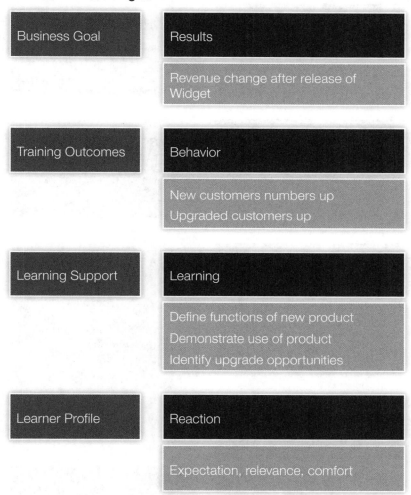

Business Goal

Results

Revenue change after release of Widget

Training Outcomes

Behavior

New customers numbers up
Upgraded customers up

Learning Support

Learning

Define functions of new product
Demonstrate use of product
Identify upgrade opportunities

Learner Profile

Reaction

Expectation, relevance, comfort

3. Match evaluation "what" with "how" will we measure.

Results	*Level 4*
Revenue change after release of Widget	Revenue from Widget Xtra

Behavior	*Level 3*
New customers numbers up Upgraded customers up	Data review Observation

Learning	*Level 2*
Define functions of new product Demonstrate use of product Identify upgrade opportunities	Test Simulate Role-play

Reaction	*Level 1*
Expectation, relevance, comfort	Survey

Design With the End in Mind—ABCD Objectives

Learning objectives are a lot like steering systems in cars. When well tuned, they simply fade into the driving experience. On the other hand, if they're just a little off-balance, you will be spending time and effort making little corrections frequently.

Objectives are traditionally written in "ABCD" format.

A. Audience–Who is the audience?

B. Behavior–What skills will be acquired?

C. Condition–What parameters are involved?

D. Degree–What constitutes success?

Examples	ABCD Breakdown
Given a compass, the scuba navigation class participant will find a location 20 meters away and return to the dive boat within 35 minutes.	A – Scuba navigation class participant B – Find a location and return to the dive boat C – Given a compass, location 20 meters away D – Within 35 minutes
The customer service representative will choose the most appropriate product offerings for a customer, given a sample customer information report.	A – Customer service rep B – Choose a product offering C – Given a sample customer information report D – Most appropriate offerings
Given the Trust Prescriptives handout, each team member will correctly identify the trust issues within the team and create a realistic action plan for resolution.	A – Team member B – Identify trust issues, create action plan C – Given the handout D – Correctly, realistic

Real-World Shortcut:

You can skip the "A" and "C" portions of objective writing if your analysis was done well, and if you design the training to be as much like real conditions as possible. Depending on the behavior and content, you may be able to skip the "D" section as well, leaving you to focus on the "B"ehavior. The "B" portion of the objectives is the most critical part!

The following examples are written as bulleted objectives after a sentence stem such as, "By the end of the training workshop, you will be able to…"

Examples	ABCD Breakdown
• **Write and discuss quarterly performance reviews with your direct reports** • **Document reviews within the Performance System** • **Conduct an annual talent overview of your team**	A – Class participant (assumption) B – Write, discuss, document reviews, and conduct talent overview C – Normal operating modes for behavior (assumption) D – Done within legal and policy guidelines (assumption)
• **Operate the Acme200x specialized tool** • **Create 400 functional widgets**	A – Class participant (assumption) B – Operate tool, create widgets C – Normal operating modes for behavior (assumption) D – Functional widgets

More information on levels of application are available on the *Real World Training Design* website.

Design With the End in Mind—Levels of Application

Writing the "B" (behavior) portion of a learning objective takes more than randomly choosing a verb. The action has to match the level of application needed for a performance change. The more complex the behavior, the more advanced the application has to be during your training project.

Behavior matching is very important to retaining new knowledge and skills. If a person needs to take apart and repair a machine for her job, asking her to simply "identify" parts on a diagram is not a true test of her skills.

Some examples:

Analysis Output	Examples	Appropriate Behaviors
Knowledge	Grocery store cashier receives training on new produce codes	List, identify, recite
Comprehension	Recently promoted warehouse manager needs to be proactive about workplace safety	Distinguish, interpret, predict
Application	Payroll professional must calculate vacation time for employees	Demonstrate, compute, show, solve
Analysis	Technician is in charge of repairing broken equipment in a plant	Analyze, break down, select
Synthesis	Branch manager of a sales company is tasked with improving the inventory process	Create, reconstruct, revise
Evaluation	An executive assistant must select the best vendor for a new software package	Appraise, compare, evaluate

Work Smarter, Not Longer—Version Controls and Naming Conventions

If you are lucky enough to work collaboratively on your training projects, there are some basic document control processes that you can put in place to save time. We've all been in a situation where we are working on a project and find out that we either don't have the latest version of a document, or, we need a certain file and have to wait for someone to come back from a meeting–or vacation.

To save yourself some headache, and some significant time, decide on the following procedures before you kick off your project:

1. Naming Files

    a. Decision Points:
        i.   lowercase? CAPITALS? Title Case?
        ii. Underscores (_) or spaces ( )? (Spaces in filenames can occasionally cause problems in certain systems.)
        iii. Avoid at all costs: *Final, Old, New*, people's names!

    b. Examples:
        i.   NewLeaderTraining_AnalysisResults_10092011.xlsx
        ii. Teamdynamics_Development_FacGuide_ver101.docx

2. Version Controls

    a. Decision Points:
        i.   Numbering system? How will you increment numbers?
        ii. Date system? What is the date format?

    b. Examples:
        i.   Version 1.01, Version 001, Version 225, Version A1
        ii. 10092011, Oct2011, 10.11, etc.

3. File Storage

    a. Decision Points:
        i.   Where will the master files be kept?
        ii. How will backups occur?

    b. Examples:
        i.   All master files are kept on a shared network drive. Files must be updated with new versions/dates each time they are worked on. The project manager backs up files to an external hard drive weekly.

$ Toll Lanes: Cost Constraints

The most difficult challenge in justifying the cost of a training design project is all of the time spent talking, thinking, and analyzing, without a lot of deliverables to show for it. These techniques will help you save money, as well as justify the funds you are able to secure.

1. Choose Wisely–This step is all about decisions. The wrong decision makes money fly out of your wallet!

    a. The Right Training Intervention

    b. Spend on the Experience

    c. Using WIIFM

2. Reduce, Reuse, Recycle–Use your resources!

    a. Reduce "Moving Parts"

    b. Reuse Templates

    c. Recycling Activities

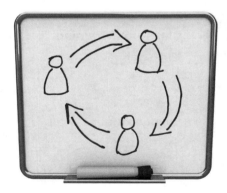

Choose Wisely—The Right Training Intervention

The art of instructional design comes down to decisions. In the case of choosing the best training intervention that will be cost-effective, there are many options.

Here is a listing of the most popular training structures, with some key considerations. Cost factors listed do not include loss of productivity.

Method	Description
Classroom Training (Off-site)	Traditional training format, facilitated learning in a group setting away from job
Classroom Training (On-site)	Traditional training format, facilitated learning in a group work setting
Asynchronous/ Self-Study	Self-paced digital and/or workbook
Synchronous/ Virtual Training	Facilitated live online class format

Remember	Direct Cost Factors
Face-to-face facilitation can make it easier to develop a sense of community and evaluate participant needs Location away from work site can increase engagement	• Participant travel, lodging, food • Location costs • Equipment rentals or shipping • Facilitator fee and expenses • Train-the-trainer costs
Face-to-face facilitation to develop intact teams and evaluate participant needs Reduces travel time, time off the job	• Participant food • Equipment rentals or shipping • Facilitator fee and expenses • Train-the-trainer costs
Learner chooses pace, focuses on most relevant learning objects at the moment Loses benefits of expert-facilitator	• Technology costs • Materials shipping • Help resources may be required
Time away from job is minimal Some benefit of expert-facilitator and community Not all learners engage well in a virtual environment	• Technology costs • Facilitator fee • Materials shipping (if applicable) • Train-the-trainer costs

Method	Description
On-the-Job Training	Just-in-time approach to training includes job aids, mobile learning, other digital media
On-the-Job Coach/ Mentor	An expert mentor teaches learner in real time
General Coach/Mentor	A mentor works with learner to determine learning objectives and plan
Learning Support Resources/Job Aids	Job aids and other performance support aids
Social Learning	Community-generated content, searchable and rated by learners

Remember	Direct Cost Factors
Learner determines content most relevant to current situation Learning is "chunked" to provide the most potential for retention Difficult to evaluate	• Technology costs • Materials shipping • Content or software FAQ resources may be required
Learner and mentor agree which content is most relevant to current situation High retention due to just-in-time format/expert facilitator Difficult to evaluate	• Technology costs • Materials shipping • Train-the-mentor costs • Mentor compensation • Content or software FAQ resources may be required
Learner and mentor agree on development plan Individualized attention and accountability May be difficult to standardize learning	• Travel and lodging may be required for meetings • Train-the-mentor costs • Mentor compensation • Support materials shipping
Help when the learner needs it Addresses many knowledge and procedure-based performance problems Rarely works for complex learning Good design is key to effectiveness	• Materials creation and shipping
Wisdom of the masses can lead to more complete content resources Content is continually vetted through the community Searchable for most relevant chunks of information Community is encouraged Social learning systems are well used across most generations Stigmas about "wastes of time" and the need to monitor content	• Technology costs • Monitoring/technology administrator costs

Choose Wisely—Spend on the Experience

Think back on the most effective and impactful learning experiences you have had in your lifetime. What was it about the learning that made it so memorable? Design components such as having a prepared facilitator, creating helpful learning materials, and planning engaging activities are what matter in the end.

When cost is the driving constraint on your project you can still create an effective learning experience for your training participants. Here are some components to think about when designing your training program. This is a subjective list based on how well these components are usually done–you should build your own dashboard reflecting your organization.

Deal Breakers
Always Worth It

- Prepared, Expert Facilitators
- Materials/Graphics Proofread
- Technology Tested, Practiced
- Experiential Activities to Engage Learners
- Follow-Up Materials for Reinforcement

Situational
50/50 Odds

- Professional Materials/Graphics
- Ice Breakers, After Break Activities
- Pre-Work Exercises
- Guest Speakers

Skip it
Cut Costs Here

- Expensive Food and Snacks
- Upgrades: Wireless Internet for Meeting Room, etc.
- Dated Video Clips, Sound Clips, Picture Slideshows
- Give-Aways, Fiddle Toys, Prizes

Choose Wisely—Using WIIFM

Here is the problem with learning objectives—we (training professionals) use them as crutches. We think that if we throw the objectives up on a slide at the beginning of a training event, the participants should immediately understand the relevance of the training to their job. That just isn't the case.

If your participants don't see the relevance of the training, you lose all of the potential value of the event. It is important to review your design for the "WIIFM": "What's in it for me?"

Ask yourself:

1. Are the learning objectives presented passively (written on a flip chart) or actively (ask learners to rate, comment, choose most important one, and so forth)?

2. Does the learner identify why he is attending this specific training early on?

3. Is the connection between the learning objectives and the organizational goals clear *to the learner*?

4. As each objective is covered during the training, does the learner have a chance to ask, "WIIFM?" and establish relevance?

5. Is there time for reviewing key points of the training before extended breaks (long refreshment breaks, lunches, overnight, between events)?

6. Will the learner have a clear idea of what *to do* in order to apply his new knowledge and skills on the job?

7. Are experiential learning activities followed by a skilled debrief or reflection in which the activity is tied concretely to objectives?

Reduce, Reuse, Recycle—Reduce "Moving Parts"

Save money in your budget by getting rid of logistical obstacles. Keeping things simple will help the training run smoothly, which has an impact on your learners.

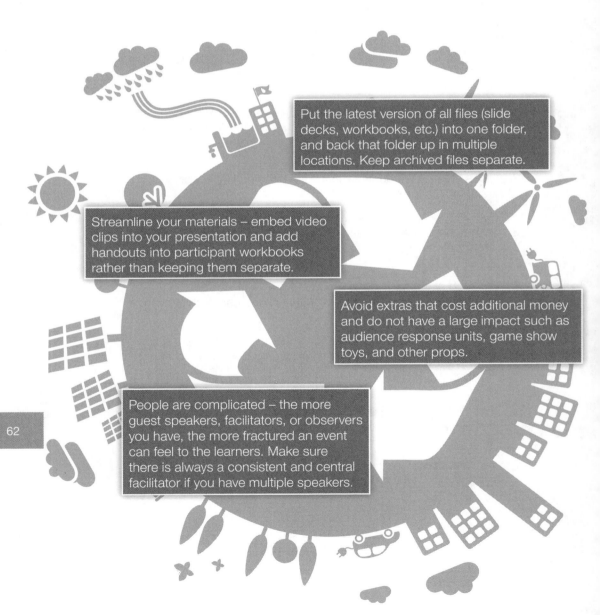

Put the latest version of all files (slide decks, workbooks, etc.) into one folder, and back that folder up in multiple locations. Keep archived files separate.

Streamline your materials – embed video clips into your presentation and add handouts into participant workbooks rather than keeping them separate.

Avoid extras that cost additional money and do not have a large impact such as audience response units, game show toys, and other props.

People are complicated – the more guest speakers, facilitators, or observers you have, the more fractured an event can feel to the learners. Make sure there is always a consistent and central facilitator if you have multiple speakers.

Reduce, Reuse, Recycle—Reuse Templates

We all know we should use templates, but most of us never get around to creating them. If you want to save significant budget and time on your projects–make templates a priority!

Template	Hot Tips
Surveys	• Create a master analysis survey and a master evaluation survey. • Each survey should contain a pool of questions that are pre-vetted for effectiveness. • When ready to use the survey, copy it, remove unnecessary questions, and make slight text changes.
Observation Form	• Create a template that has instructions about objective observation. • Tool should be able to be used by non-learning professionals as well as trained facilitators. • Choose a Likert scale (1 to 5, etc.) that your organization will use, and stick to it for all rated questions.
Analysis Results Deliverable	• Create a branded template to deliver analysis results to your stakeholders. • Include four categories (business goals, learning outcomes, learning support, learner profile).
Evaluation Plan	• Includes objectives of the training. • Use space to address what will be measured in levels 1 to 4.
Storyboard	• Include pieces of the training, where each objective is addressed, learner engagement points, and timing.

Reduce, Reuse, Recycle—Recycling Activities

Why reinvent the wheel? Recycle your training activities! Sometimes we get caught up in needing to come up with all-new learning experiences–but ask yourself, Is that for the learner? Or for you? You may have seen the card-sort activity 200 times, but your learners haven't!

You can create a stockpile of experiential learning activities and employ them with different audiences, materials, or instructions to keep them fresh. Change the debrief of the activity to point out important information.

Example: Gallery Walk

Basics: Set up flip chart paper around the classroom. Each page should be titled with a different idea corresponding to the activity (for example, Leader Characteristics, Great Leaders, Leadership Styles). Participants (individually or in small groups) rotate past each flip chart adding their own thoughts to the page.

Variations: 1. Allow more time in the first round and task groups with creating an exhaustive list. Then have subsequent groups rate the options rather than adding their own. 2. Instruct participants to add to charts at each break. 3. Write participant names on each chart. Have participants write kudos on each other's charts during the training event.

⚠ Scenic Route: Quality or Scope Constraints

If quality or compliance is your greatest constraint, the design process is going to be where you earn your stripes. Investing the time during this stage helps to pave the way for the rest of the project. During this time, you should focus on following well-vetted models and guidelines and using the systems already imbedded in the organization to guarantee an effective training project.

1. Stand on the Shoulders of Giants–There are oodles of learning models available to you to make sure you are designing the most effective training possible.

    a. Effective Learning Styles

    b. Training Outlines

2. What's Happening?–Do you know the systemic leverage points in your organization? Utilize the ways that people interact to increase the learning potential of your training.

    a. Communication–Who, When, and How Often

    b. A Brief Diversion Into Informal Learning

On the Shoulders of Giants—Learning Styles

Learning styles have been around for quite a while. Many people involved in training can tell you whether they are a visual, auditory, or kinesthetic (movement) learner. Unfortunately, many L&D professionals put too much stock in the idea of learning preferences. Like many of the models in the training world, the best way to view learning styles is as a reminder to create engaging training.

Integrate all three modes of learning into your training design. Make sure that you are providing visualized information, providing auditory learning, and creating movement-based experiences. It's best to create a varied approach—no matter who your learners are. The following chart provides some ideas of how to vary your content across the different learning styles.

Visual	Auditory	Kinesthetic
Use different colors, shapes, and icons to represent different ideas.	**Use a questioning method of facilitation to engage learners on subjects.**	Walk and learn (as a group, go to the C-Suite to discuss the company's mission, stop by reception to talk about customer service, etc.).
Have participants depict what they have learned on flip charts with words or pictures.	**Use brainstorming activities in small groups and share back verbally to larger groups.**	Provide fiddle toys, puzzles, magnets, or pipecleaners to keep participants' hands busy.
Ask learners to visualize the results of learning new skills. Visualization is a powerful tool.	**Have learners create slogans, jingles, or mnemonics for lesson takeaways.**	Use Post-it notes or index cards in "card sort" or prioritization activities.
Laminate job aids and performance support tools as class takeaways.	**In pairs or triads, conduct role-plays. A third person can be an observer and provide feedback.**	Get participants out of their seats for icebreakers, closers, and all breaks.

On the Shoulders of Giants—Training Outlines

After you have a storyboard, but before you begin creating a participant guide, it is important to create a training outline. Outlines are a great incremental way to build the training program—and provide a deliverable you can share with your stakeholders to validate your progress.

The storyboard step of the design process lets you create "chunks" of training that address your learning objectives. The first general outline takes this design one step further—adding slight detail around each content piece. This outline contains only high-level information to share with stakeholders. A subject matter expert (SME) or executive could read this version of the outline and understand the basic flow of the training, what is covered, and what types of learning activities will be included.

DAY 1 - TUESDAY

Show "parts" of the class, length, and who will facilitate.

INTRODUCTIONS
30 mins, Facilitator
- ▶ Discussion: Leadership Development Life Cycle
- ▶ Purpose of class, Agenda
- ▶ Introduce VP of Sales

Give key talking points.

KICK-OFF
30 mins, Vice President of Sales

Break

Information about class breaks, lunches, and flow.

PRE-WORK REVIEW
45 mins, Facilitator
- ▶ Purpose: Determine the most critical areas for improvement and focus on impact.
- ▶ Discussion: Reading assessments, prioritizing results
- ▶ Workbook: Form for compiling and prioritizing multiple assessment results
- ▶ Partner Work: Self-Development (Step One of Action Plan)
  - · What are my strengths? How do they compare to core competencies?
  - · What are my most urgent areas for improvement?
  - · How do these gaps affect me as a leader?

Include every activity with objectives, instructions, and debrief points.

Include usage of workbooks, presentations, and other media.

68

The second, more detailed outline, gets much more granular. This outline is the pre-cursor to creating the training materials. You will want to document all of your details in this version–which makes it a little too much to share with stakeholders. The purpose is to keep yourself organized throughout the design step, and to make the transition from design to development easy!

DAY 1 - TUESDAY

Show "parts" of the class, length, and who will facilitate.

INTRODUCTIONS
8:00am – 8:30am, Facilitator
- ▸ Objective: Communicate class purpose and agenda, set the tone and environment for the week.
- ▸ Discussion: Leadership Development Life Cycle

Give key talking points.

What did it take for you to get here? Why now? Explain facilitator's journey to leadership. Talk about failures as well as success. (Show Slide 1)
Instruct class to take notes in workbook.
Set up the purpose of the week.
- ▸ Purpose of Class:
  - • WIIFL? Draw out participant answers. (Show Slide 2)
- ▸ Agenda:
  - • Review the agenda and have each participant identify one or more topics that they believe will have the largest impact on their business.
  - • Workbook: Participants begin action plan and identify personal learning objectives.
- ▸ Introduce VP of Sales
  - • Brief introduction, refer to workbook notes page.

Include usage of workbooks, presentations, and other media.

KICK-OFF
8:30-9:00am, VP of Sales
- ▸ Objective: Consider alignment between "Good to Great" and onboarding leadership.
- ▸ Facilitated Lecture: Good to Great
  - • Re-cap pre-class reading of "Good to Great." Discuss alignment.
- ▸ Executive Sponsorshi
  - • VP should underline her sponsorship of the leadership development class to increase engagement by learners.

PRE-WORK REVIEW
9:00am – 9:45am, Marie Curie
- ▸ Objective: Determine the most critical a
  impact.
- ▸ Discussion: Reading assessments, prio

Only include detail when it is needed to understand the activity. Be careful not to go too deep during this step.

What's Happening?—Communication: Who, When, and How Often?

If there is one rule about working with your clients or stakeholders, it's this: Communicate early and often. Here are some guidelines. You will want to create a communication plan for each of your projects to make sure this crucial piece of training success doesn't get forgotten!

Hype a new training event the correct way. Get "headliners" involved early to get even more people excited about the event.

Stakeholders:

Continue your weekly or biweekly meetings to keep your clients informed of progress and problems.

Provide deliverables such as storyboards, training outlines, and materials as they are completed to prevent surprises later on!

Learning & Development Team:

Conduct frequent, but efficient team status checks to make sure progress is continuing.

Encourage peer reviews of design deliverables and materials to ensure the highest-quality product.

Learners:

Begin a marketing campaign during the design phase of the project. Share information such as guest speakers, inclusion of social or online learning components, and competencies covered to build anticipation.

Managers:

Don't forget about your learners' bosses. Communicate to managers what behavior changes they should expect to see and how they can support performance back on the job. Remember that you need manager buy-in to see a true change in performance.

What's Happening?—A Brief Diversion Into Informal Learning

Many books have been written about informal learning. However, any conversation about quality constraints on training design would be remiss if it didn't at least address informal learning.

So, what is it? Informal learning is basically when an individual acquires knowledge and skills from his or her job, peers, or community. This is the learning that happens because learners need to know how to do their job, run into problems that need to be solved, and proactively seek self-development (in many forms). Learning that is organic to the job–and to our nature as social beings–is a fundamental part of how we grow.

Most experts agree that formal directed learning, for example, the kind that you are working on right now, doesn't hold a candle to informal learning when it comes to effectiveness and retention. But don't despair–that doesn't mean that formal learning is obsolete. The new reality of workforce development means that we have to consider the effects of informal learning in our design process.

To get more of a handle on this huge, and very crucial, topic please refer to the recommended reading in appendix A.

TOP 10 THINGS ABOUT INFORMAL LEARNING

1	Informal learning is not a new concept, and it is not a trend that will disappear. People have been learning from others on an as-needed basis far longer than they have been sitting in classrooms.
2	The ability for people to learn what they need, when they need it, results in high retention rates for knowledge and skills.
3	Social learning—an aspect of informal learning—is identified by content that is co-created by community participants. Knowledge is built through collaboration.
4	During your analysis, identify points of strong informal learning. Where do people acquire their skills? How are behaviors formed? What are the "unwritten rules"? Consider how this affects your training program.
5	Informal learning is by definition, unstructured. Attempting to "formalize" or put controls in place changes the dynamic of those interactions. Rather than attempting to manage it, embrace and encourage that kind of development.

6 Millennials, and young generations, are not the only ones benefiting from informal or social learning. Everyone wants to be engaged, and participate in a community regardless of age. If you show the WIIFM, the crowds will follow.

7 Utilizing informal learning means providing effective means of searching for content, creating and sharing information, and building communities through social learning. The outcomes are increased productivity, more learning, and higher retention of skills and knowledge.

8 The benefits of informal learning technologies (such as social networking, blogging, and wikis) extend beyond just-in-time learning and retention. Reflection and peer feedback are also built into the process and increase the potential for learning by multitudes.

9 True informal learning is not achieved through implementation of a moderated blog with required postings. Understand what systems are already in use, and which systems can increase the natural workflow of your learners.

10 Informal learning really comes down to increasing performance. If you understand that the end goal is a behavior change that leads to results, and that sitting in a classroom is not the only way to get there, you are on the right path.

⊗ Tour Guide: A Design for High Expectations

Elaine Biech, ebb associates inc.
editor, *The ASTD Leadership Handbook*

Cruzin is a privately-held young manufacturing company with 200 employees that had been in business for three years when it contacted me. I was excited to work with Cruzin because most of the companies I work with have been in business a long time, some over 100 years. Although I was excited about the opportunity to have a new company without any "bad habits," what I did not anticipate was the challenge of delivering services while at the same time putting processes in place to implement those services.

The second challenge was that the company did not have a strategic plan–honest! I'd never worked with an organization that did not have at least a few corporate goals. Cruzin's goal was to "make money." That's it. The company was doing a good job of it too. It did not hire me initially to conduct strategic planning, but to design a training program for its employees because it wanted to "keep them engaged, educated, and happy."

The third challenge was managing the company's high expectations for the employee development effort. You may be thinking, "Give me some of those 'high expectations' any day!" Cruzin's leaders expected customized training, in a minimum amount of time, at very little cost.

The organization's entrepreneurial leaders were adamant that this was not the time to conduct strategic planning, but that it was imperative to invest in people and their development. They believed that:

- Since all the leaders came from different companies, there was a need to build a common language.

- To grow the company, they needed to develop their people —immediately.

- It was important to do what's right by investing in the company's people.

- Everyone needed to work better as a team to drive success.
- Basics such as improving communication were common sense and did not need a strategic plan.

To establish a baseline and direction we interviewed a cross section of 59 employees to determine what competencies they believed were most critical to shape and sustain the future of the company and to "make money." To save time we asked interviewees to prioritize 49 commonly accepted leadership competencies. The employees identified 12 incredibly consistent competencies that were further substantiated by their stories. The competencies were synthesized into five key categories for management ease:

- teamwork (trust, relationships)
- communication (exercising influence, managing conflict, styles, flexibility)
- leading change (communication, building trust)
- strategic planning (planning for the future)
- developing others (delegating, empowering, identifying talent).

In a half-day session Cruzin's leadership team designed a plan for tying the goal of "make money" to measurable results and identified the behaviors employees would need to exhibit. For example, when communication and conflict management were discussed, the results the team expected to see were a reduction of re-work and errors; the behaviors required would be an increase in planning across departments and reduced complaining. In most cases it was easy to develop the design objectives from this input.

During the interviews we discovered one employee who had started a "library" and had already designed and conducted training for his people. Several others used communication models that they adapted for their employees. Rather than introduce a new set of jargon, or create new content, we started with what was available and built from there. Through the interviews, we also identified several potential trainers.

During this first year, Cruzin was able to deliver one new topic every month to employees. This was possible because we developed repeatable processes that saved time in the long run. In addition, the designs for each topic followed a template that was reused. The results, behaviors, and objectives were defined, discussed, and presented up front; employees knew why they were there and what behavior was expected. Although there was a design template, there was no "time template." Programs ranged from 75 minutes to 7 hours and 50 minutes. The mantra was "take the time required, no more, no less," which saved time overall.

Three other sources saved design time. First, employees continued to voluntarily offer critical incidents, role-plays, and problems that were built into the designs. They would come to us saying, "I don't know where this will fit, but here's a situation that occurs over and over on the floor." This ensured the content was customized for Cruzin, strengthened the WIIFM, saved time in design, and most importantly, kept employees involved in the training efforts. Second, we tapped into books that published customizable activities. This saved design time. Our favorite resources were *The Pfeiffer Annuals* (Wiley), *The Ten-Minute Trainer* (Pfeiffer), *Developing Great Managers* (ASTD), and *90 World-Class Activities by 90 World-Class Trainers* (Pfeiffer). Third, one of the employees attended ASTD's International Conference & Exposition (ICE) soon after we started the design where she met a trainer from another manufacturing company. The two of them regularly exchanged ideas and content that each customized to her own needs.

Critical to the design was a laminated Employee Workspace Guide that incorporated all the key points from each training session. Instead of employees balancing a dozen three-ring binders, they have a single laminated page that represents each topic. Follow-on coaching was also available for every employee to ensure that the expected behavior was clearly understood and implemented by each learner. This may not have saved time during design, but it certainly ensured return on expectation.

While Cruzin started out to be one of my greatest training challenges, it also resulted in an exceptional success story. The template used for design was soon enhanced and used for rapid online learning. Online learning is offered as synchronous and recorded for future asynchronous training. The laminated Employee Workspace Guides evolved into a tablet format. It has become a badge of accomplishment for an employee to graduate from the laminated guides to receive his/her own electronic tablet. Most employees are involved in either the design or delivery of training, accepting continuous learning for all as a part of their normal workday.

Cruzin's high expectations were never compromised. The company knew the value of high quality. It demanded customized design so that employees could immediately see relationships to their work at Cruzin. And the company expected the design to provide time to process activities and to allow participants time to experience the WIIFM. Cruizin is designing its own employee development now, and continues to save design time by contacting me occasionally for new resources, ideas, or contacts.

By the way, Cruzin eventually developed a strategic plan. Its leaders found that much of the work I had required them to do before developing their training design model was actually a productive step toward developing their strategic plan. Over the past four years the company has had a very low turnover rate in their industry. It has satisfied employees, and a flourishing customer base that helps the company "make money." Cruzin had high expectations of what employee development could accomplish, and it achieved what it expected.

⛽ Fuel Up: Chapter Exercise: Analysis–Design Map

(Using Learning Objectives)

In the form provided, write out the key findings from your audience and content analysis. Use what you have learned from this chapter to document the impact of those findings on your training design. Use the chart on page 46 for help.

Analysis Output	Design Considerations	Impact on Your Design
Business Goal	Alignment w/ business goals Provide strategic value	
Training Outcomes	Behavior change as a result of trainings	
Learning Support	Specific skills and knowledge content to change behavior	
Learner Profile	Learner characteristics such as motivators, obstacles	
(Other findings)		

⛽ Fuel Up: Chapter Tool: Storymap

The entire storymap tool is available in the appendix of the book, as well as through the *Real World Training Design* website.

Training Design Storyboard

LEARNER PROFILE:

Use your audience analysis to determine key characteristics of your learners. These are the top ideas that need to be taken into consideration when designing your training.

Relevance	Expectation	Obstacles
What knowledge and skills do learners gain from this training? How will this training solve a problem for the learner?	Is this a required training? What communication has been sent out regarding training? How have learners been prepared for the training?	What systems, management, policies, or cultural issues may prevent the learner from applying new skills and knowledge? (Could be perceptions or reality)

Training Design Storyboard

BUSINESS RESULTS:

Identify the business issues that the training will address. Use strategic, organizational language rather than learning language.

Goal 1:	Goal 2:	Goal 3:
What is the primary business goal for this training?	What are the business goals for this training?	What are the business goals for this training?
What is the strategic result that this training will help achieve?	What is the strategic result that this training will help achieve?	What is the strategic result that this training will help achieve?

LEARNING OUTCOMES:

List the specific behaviors that will change as a result of this training. These behaviors should align with the business goals, and take into account the learner profile above.

Learning Outcome 1	Learning Outcome 2	Learning Outcome 3
What are the specific job tasks that will change or improve as a result of this training? How will behavior change?	What are the specific job tasks that will change or improve as a result of this training? How will behavior change?	What are the specific job tasks that will change or improve as a result of this training? How will behavior change?

Training Design Storyboard

LEARNING OBJECTIVES

List the terminal and enabling objectives of this training. Use observable, measurable verbs. Number the objectives.

Knowledge	Skills	Attitudes
Define, describe, identify, memorize, name, state, recall, predict, solve, relate	Apply, demonstrate, change, modify, operate, practice, produce, show, use, write	Analyze, distinguish, examine, illustrate, infer, interpret, compose, summarize, tell, write

Training Design Storyboard

DESIGN FACTORS:

For each storyboard box, indicate whether there will be an intellectual or emotional component to that section of the training. Indicate which objective each section addresses. Finally, draw the energy line across the flow of the training to make sure you are managing the energy and ntensity of the class.

Intellectual	Energy Line	Emotional
• Examples, testimony • Data, evidence, proof • Logical argument • Exhibits, props • Case studies		• Story • Metaphor, anecdote, parable • Thought-provoking question • Shock or surprise • Humor

DEVELOPMENT

To create something exceptional, your mindset must be relentlessly focused on the smallest detail.

-Giorgio Armani

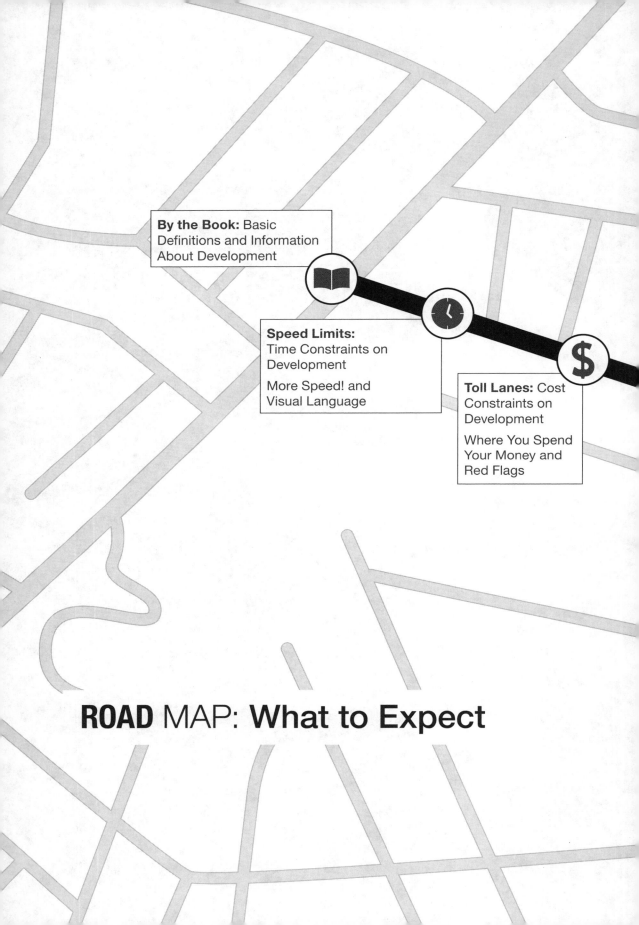

By the Book: Basic Definitions and Information About Development

Speed Limits: Time Constraints on Development

More Speed! and Visual Language

Toll Lanes: Cost Constraints on Development

Where You Spend Your Money and Red Flags

ROAD MAP: What to Expect

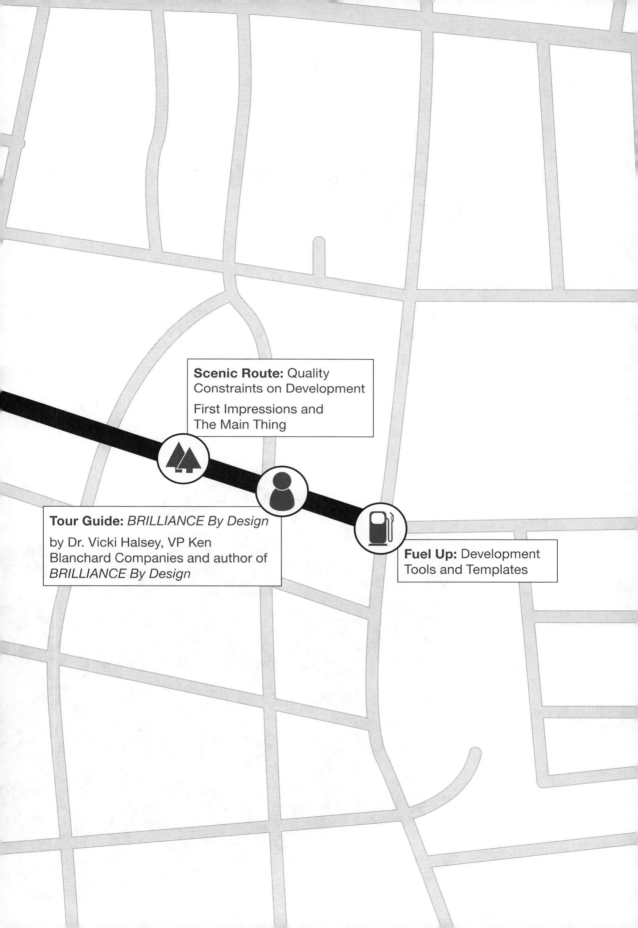

Scenic Route: Quality Constraints on Development

First Impressions and The Main Thing

Tour Guide: *BRILLIANCE By Design*

by Dr. Vicki Halsey, VP Ken Blanchard Companies and author of *BRILLIANCE By Design*

Fuel Up: Development Tools and Templates

Development: Packing Your Bags

Well—you know where you're going, how you're getting there, and who's going with you. Now it's time to fold up those Bermuda shorts, dig out the sunscreen, and pack your extra sandals!

The development phase is where ideas start to take shape through material creation, e-learning components, and social learning technology. Development includes everything from building participant guides to shooting video to quality-checking online content.

📖 By the Book: Development

The development phase of the ADDIE process is the most tangible and easily measured. The goal during this phase is to create all of the materials and deliverables needed for your training event. This is also the time when you will begin preparing your facilitators (if they're not you!).

Key Considerations:

- Web-based learning content and platform
- Participant materials:
    ▶ Participant guides, job aids, digital content, pre-work
- Facilitator materials:
    ▶ Instructor guides, quick-glance cards, presentations, handouts
- Evaluation materials such as surveys, observation checklists, charts

The development phase must include enough time and resources to build all materials needed, as well as review, edit, and update those materials. There should be time allotted for quality assurance on any web-based learning content, or technology-assisted learning.

⏱ Speed Limits: Time Constraints

Product development life cycles across all industries are shrinking. It doesn't matter if you make mobile phones or mini cheeseburgers, your customers expect them faster than ever. This is definitely true of training materials development. From your customer's perspective, all you are doing is making a "pretty" workbook–why would it take more than a couple of days? There are a few ways for all training professionals to take up the slack during the development phase of the project.

1. More Speed!–There are all sorts of new models out there for quick turnaround times in both e-learning and classroom training development.

    a. Rapid Development

    b. Working With SMEs

2. Visual Language–Save time by writing less and drawing more. Adult learners are far more likely to hear your message if it's visual.

    a. Interesting Numbers

More Speed!—Rapid Development

There is a lot of information out there about rapid instructional design or rapid development; however, the basis of this philosophy is really about *iterative design*.

The idea is to have parallel workflows in which modular components of the training are in their own development cycle. The results of each cycle acts as input to the training design as a whole.

This process works really well for some projects because it allows you to develop a piece of the puzzle, test it out, and adjust as you go, rather than waiting until the entire training project is developed to find out if you were on track or not.

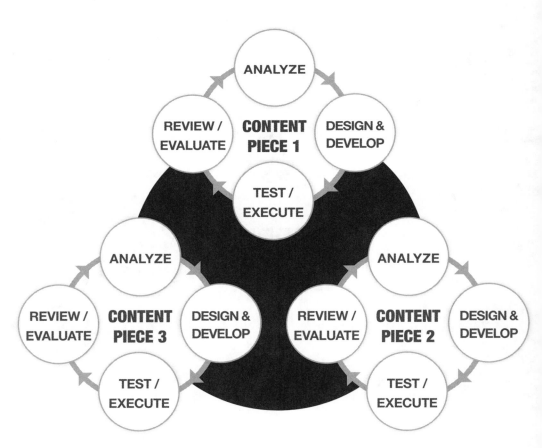

Practice caution with this process. Rapid development requires the training project to be "chunkable." Let's say you are developing a workshop on performance management conversations, where the content builds on foundational knowledge (policies and procedures) to advanced content (how to craft your message). It's nearly impossible to take just the last activity and pilot that with a group of test subjects!

Well, then, how do you determine the "chunks" of your training project? Simple! Make sure that your objectives are clearly defined–they usually represent the pieces of a training project. Utilize the storyboard tool from the design chapter to create logical pieces for this process.

Training Design Storyboard

LEARNING OBJECTIVES

List the terminal and enabling objectives of this training. Use observable, measurable verbs. Number the objectives.

Knowledge	Skills	Attitudes
Define, describe, identify, memorize, name, state, recall, predict, solve, relate	Apply, demonstrate, change, modify, operate, practice, produce, show, use, write	Analyze, distinguish, examine, illustrate, infer, interpret, compose, summarize, tell, write

More Speed!—Working With SMEs

One of the major misconceptions about ISD is that designers need to know a lot about their course content in order to create a great product–and that just isn't true. Instructional designers are adult learning experts, learner advocates, and system thinkers–they rely on SMEs (subject matter experts) to provide the specific nuggets of content, and then the designer uses the content to create an impactful learning experience.

Unfortunately, the process of working with SMEs can be frustrating and time-consuming. Here are some tips for saving yourself time, and lowering your blood pressure:

1. Be Aware of Territory Lines–Many working relationships get off on the wrong foot and create disagreeable circumstances for completing a project. Understand that SMEs, by definition, are experts in something and give them the respect they deserve. They are your partners, not underlings who live to provide you with content.

2. Run, Drive, and Row in the Same Direction–Establish the project goals up front. Explain to your SMEs that you are all trying to achieve the same results. You may want to show them your evaluation plan to show the impact that you all, as a team, are trying to make.

3. Don't Look Like a Tourist–Credibility is important. Describe what you do (as an ISD, HR professional, etc.) and why you have the expertise needed to work on this project. Explain your role (again as a project manager, designer, and so forth–not a content expert.) However, you will want to be very careful about this conversation so it does not look like boasting.

4. Learn the Language–Listen carefully to the vocabulary and jargon used by your SMEs and try to speak the same language. This clears up miscommunication, shows that you are listening and learning, and helps puts your SMEs at ease.

5. Carry a Map–Set the expectation of the SMEs up front. What kind of information will you expect from them? In what format will you want it? How much time and effort should they expect to spend on this project? Why should they?

6. Thank You in Any Language–When a SME contributes content, attends your meetings, and so forth, make sure you thank them honestly. The world of training would suffer greatly without our SMEs.

Visual Language—Interesting Numbers

As an industry, training (or learning and development), has a large blind spot. We have grown so much in terms of becoming better business partners and measuring impact, in providing engaging learning experiences, and facilitating well.

However, our materials are stuck in word processor limbo. Sitting through our slides is like seeing someone walking around in a "Duran Duran" t-shirt and stonewashed jeans. Yikes.

Put another way, when you put up a slide like this:

Where is our company going?

Increase market share.

We expect to gain 5% market share across all of our North Ameican operations.

New service lines.

Rolling out three new lines of service over the next six months to increase out ability to meet customer needs.

Focus on customer service.

Hold every employee accountable for the highest caliber of customer service. Measured annually.

You make people feel like this:

So let's talk about a couple of ways you can make information interesting. There are some rules for visualizing information:

1. One Idea per Page: Whether it's a presentation, a participant guide, or an e-learning module, only show one idea at a time.

2. Facilitate, Don't Read: Your audience will read the text on the slides or the content on the page, so there's no need to read it to them. If they realize that they are getting the same information from you as in their notebook on the screen, they will tune you out!

3. Show What You Want Them to Remember: The words or images used should represent the one Big Idea that you need the participants to retain. Provide a job aid for the details.

4. Number of Pages Does Not Equal Time Spent: Believe it or not, the number of slides in your presentation does not indicate how much time you will be speaking. It is better to spend 30 seconds each on several slides showing examples than to cram all your content onto one unreadable slide.

5. Abolish Line Graphs: If you want to show statistical or number-based information, pull out the "aha" and show only that number. Your audience will get the message right away rather than trying to decipher an entire chart.

The examples below are very basic and simple ways to depict big ideas without needing a graphic artist. This is the bare minimum for making information more interesting.

You want to teach: a new onboarding process

Only depict the high-level process as a memory device. Provide the details in a document, in a job aid, or on your intranet.

The Old Way:

On-Boarding
- Pre-Hire Call
  - Schedule a 30 minute call with new hire
  - Discuss expectations for business attire, work hours
- Paperwork
  - Fill out forms A-123, ZXV76, and Acme E.C. in triplicate
- First Day
  - Have new hire read a policies manual all day long
- First Week
  - Stop in briefly to make sure employee feels welcome

The New Way:

You want to teach: a soft idea like "courage"

Use evocative imagery to hit an idea hard with the audience. Try to elicit an immediate emotional response. Avoid clichéd images when possible.

The Old Way:

The New Way:

You want to teach: projected growth

Clearly identify the number that makes a difference. Leave out the labels and other metrics that just confuse the point. If the data are compelling enough, they will speak for themselves.

The Old Way:

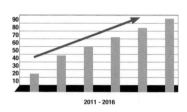

The New Way:

More on Presenting Information:

Terrific resources and tons of inspiration are available on the *Real World Training Design* website, including links to Duarte Design, Ruth Colvin Clark, and others.

$ **Toll Lanes: Cost Constraints**

Because the development step of the ADDIE process contains the most deliverables, it can also be the most costly.

Here's a phrase you will probably never hear: "Money is no object!"

We all have to deal with the reality of a tight economy and shrinking budgets. So how do you develop meaty training on a skinny budget?

1. Where You Spend Your Money—Balancing cost savings and quality when selecting and working with vendors is difficult. What questions do you ask before purchasing materials and tools?

    a. Graphic Designers and E-Learning Developers

    b. Software Applications

2. Red Flags—Slight missteps in development lead to large budget issues later. Recognizing speed bumps off in the distance, and dealing with them proactively, is a key skill of an effective designer.

    a. Common Missteps in Development

Where You Spend Your Money—Graphic Designers and E-Learning Developers

There are some things for which you should never try and find a bargain—plastic surgery, for example. However, if you are in the market for a graphic designer or a developer (whether as a contracting partner or to hire internally), there are some deals to be had.

First, I need to say that there are some designers and developers out there who charge serious money—and deserve every penny of it. These folks make your ideas look good, really good. But, if cost is the biggest issue, follow these tips to find your business partners without the hefty price tag.

FIND A GREAT DESIGNER; THEN FIND THE PEOPLE HE MENTORS.

IT IS BETTER TO FIND AN EXPERT IN ONE THING THAN TO FIND AN EXPERT IN ALL THINGS.

THERE IS GREAT, UNTAPPED TALENT AT UNIVERSITIES AND TRADE SCHOOLS.

NEVER UNDERESTIMATE THE POWER OF GUARANTEED FUTURE WORK.

REMEMBER, IT TAKES MORE MONEY TO BUILD SOMETHING BRAND NEW THAN TO REUSE EXISTING PARTS.

101

Where You Spend Your Money—Software Applications

Whether you are talking about a learning management system (LMS), a business simulation, e-learning modules, or a social learning mobile app, the cost of a software learning solution can vary widely from vendor to vendor. However, the money pit isn't in the application itself; it's all about the additional costs not included on the sales slicks.

The following list will help you to sort through vendors and choose good bets. Remember, even if someone aces this checklist, there could be hidden costs. If you have a contracts expert in your organization, ask him or her to help you with this process.

1. **Do they understand your goals?** In vendors' conversations or proposals, make sure they identify how their product will help your organization meet its goals—not just the training project goals. This can mean the difference between hiring a strategic partner and hiring an opportunistic one.

2. **Have they worked with an organization like yours before?** Find vendors who have worked with an organization the same size as yours, as well as the same type (private sector, nonprofit, and so forth). They are more likely to understand the pace and challenges faced by your project.

3. **What do their customers say?** Ask to speak to references. The references should be recent, from a similar organization, and use the exact same product. Ask the customers specifically about unanticipated costs and mistakes that cost money. Ask how quickly the vendors rectified any issues encountered, and how well they worked within budget and timeline.

> Caution! These vendors have the same goal you do—to provide a high-quality product on budget and on time. Set them up for success: Be honest about your constraints and potential road blocks.

4. **What guarantees do you have?** If cost is your biggest constraint, ask the vendors what guarantees they can provide around pricing. What is the margin of error? Ask them to be conservative with their estimates, and be honest about your tolerance for overages.

Red Flags—Common Missteps in Development

Be proactive in identifying and mitigating risks during the development phase of your training project. Small undiscovered and unanticipated issues can lead to re-work by designers, graphic artists, developers, and project managers…and all of a sudden the cost of your project can go through the roof.

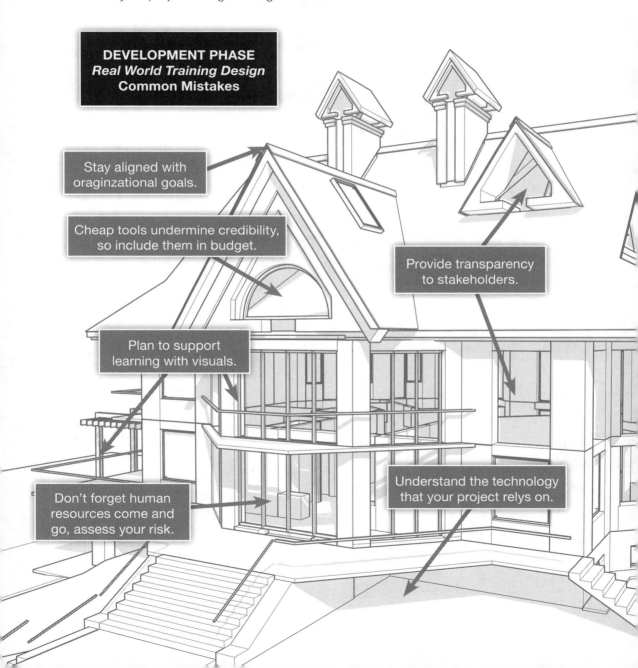

DEVELOPMENT PHASE
Real World Training Design
Common Mistakes

Stay aligned with oraginzational goals.

Cheap tools undermine credibility, so include them in budget.

Provide transparency to stakeholders.

Plan to support learning with visuals.

Don't forget human resources come and go, assess your risk.

Understand the technology that your project relys on.

⚠ Scenic Route: Quality or Scope Constraints

Remember the saying, "Anything worth doing is worth doing right"? This is the step where all of your effort in ensuring high quality begins to pay off. A targeted analysis and highly engaging design lead to effective materials development. At this stage, the potential road blocks to watch out for are around quality assurance and scope creep.

1. One Chance to Make a First Impression—Unpolished deliverables destroy the credibility of your training project. Review and quality assurance are essential.

   a. User Testing

   b. A Checklist for Review

2. The Main Thing—Don't let your project scope get larger when you aren't paying attention. Execute on your plan!

   a. Managing Your Stakeholders

One Chance to Make a First Impression—User Testing

Once upon a time, in a land not so far away, I was a young inexperienced designer. I was a rock star, and I since I did amazing work all the time, I never used spell-checker. (Do you see where this is going?) I sent out a mass emailing to about 150 top leaders in the organization with an innovative new tool for assessing talent. This is what I wrote in the email: "Please send back your assessment by the end of the week."

Guess what? I didn't say "assessment"; I abbreviated "assessment" in a very embarrassing way.

Guess what else? No one took the tool seriously as people were all too busy replying back with jokes.

The moral of this story:

> Always, always, always
> **_take the time to review documents,_**
> **_communication, and presentations_**.
> The assessment you save
> could be your own.

Ask for colleagues outside of your immediate project to review written documents for grammar, relevancy, and clarity. Test digital materials with representatives of your learner population. Test materials, activities, and learning technology as many times as you need in order to get it perfect before implementation!

One Chance to Make a First Impression—Review Checklist

Use a review checklist for all of your deliverables to ensure a typo-free implementation. You can create your own checklist, or *Review Guidance*, and provide it to each person helping with your testing or review process.

A checklist is provided at the end of this chapter in the Fuel Up: Chapter Exercise on page 115.

Remember to do a thorough quality assurance on:

- ☐ business goal alignment
- ☐ structure
- ☐ grammar/spelling
- ☐ graphics
- ☐ interfaces (if applicable)
- ☐ functionality (if applicable)

The Main Thing—Managing Your Stakeholders

At some point, you will have impressed your stakeholders so much that they may try to expand the scope of your project. It is important to look out for scope creep risk points and stay clear. Introducing new pieces to your project midstream is like jumping on a moving train—it usually doesn't end well.

Here are some suggestions for having these mission-critical conversations with your stakeholders or clients.

1. "I appreciate your vote of confidence, but I want to make sure I deliver the original high-quality product we agreed on."

Remind your stakeholders about the project charter from your kick-off meeting. Your entire team has been working hard to deliver a world-class training project within certain constraints, and it wouldn't be fair to your team or to your client to compromise the quality of your current project by adding more features, and so forth.

2. "This sounds like a great opportunity. Can we discuss this further after we launch the current project?"

There's no reason to put your foot down and turn down the work outright. Ask if you can stagger the add-on with the launch of the original product to ensure the original goals are met. Come to the table with a solution, not more problems.

3. "How does this help us reach our business goals?"

Be clear about how the expanded scope will align with business goals. Remember that your entire project so far has been aligned through extensive planning. This question alone may convince the stakeholder to drop the increased work (for now).

4. "How does this new work rank in priority with the original work?"

Maybe the expansion is mission critical after all. Let the stakeholder make that determination—but negotiate away some of the work from the original scope to still guarantee a high-quality product.

👤 Tour Guide: BRILLIANCE by Design

Dr. Vicki Halsey, VP, Ken Blanchard Companies
Author of *BRILLIANCE by Design*

The Ken Blanchard Companies® designs learning experiences so that clients feel it is their program being taught. We seamlessly thread their values and objectives throughout our content and models with a learner-centric goal of having people (both learners and facilitators) feel energized, powerful, and brilliant.

A template to ensure we design a learning experience that will help people not just feel brilliant, but also have the skills to meet organizational imperatives or objectives, is the *BRILLIANCE by Design* ENGAGE Model.

E	Energize Learners
N	Navigate Content
G	Generate Meaning
A	Apply to Real Word
G	Gauge and Celebrate
E	Extend Learning to Action

This model helps structure the flow of training and ensures that learners myelinate paths to new information in their brain through repetition, variety, practice, and active—not passive—participation. All six steps ensure the individual learner actually has developed new skills he or she will use on the job.

Adapted from the book *Brilliance by Design* by Vicki Halsey (Berrett-Koehler & ASTD Press, 2011). Used with permission.

An example of this training design is depicted below. The situation involved a global pharmaceutical company that wanted its leaders to speak the language of leadership by understanding the Situational Leadership® II model. The company's goal was to develop its sales leaders to help the sales force meet the five key drivers for the year. The company did not want its leaders to just tell people what to do; the company wanted them to be able to teach people how to successfully do what was needed. Using the People, Content, and ENGAGE model, the draft of the session to develop the pilot materials looked like this:

People (Who): Midlevel Sales Leaders	Content (What): Situational Leadership® II model
Needs: Sales reps to achieve five key drivers	Main principles or skills to master: Diagnosis, flexibility, and partnering
Objectives: Learn and apply the Situational Leadership® II model	
Information about their world: • participants are familiar with, and like, blended solutions • most are male, high Ds on DISC, extroverted, and enjoy interactivity • most are multitaskers; quick thinkers	What I want them to be able to do: 1) teach their direct reports the Situational Leadership® II model; 2) have a "well-oiled reverse gear" so as to flex their leadership styles to match the needs of their people; and 3) have follower-driven one-on-one meetings where direct reports diagnose themselves and ask for the leadership style they need.
Learning Design: ENGAGE	

E	Before Session: Focus and excite	3 weeks out: Send the SLII® article and mini study guide and 45-minute kick-off virtual classroom presentation. 0–2 weeks out: Take online asynchronous simulation teaching the main concepts of SLII® and having participants practice them.
ENERGIZE LEARNERS	Room Setup	Rounds, protein snacks, posters of SLII and leadership quotes.
	To Start Session: Thank and involve immediately	1-day classroom session opening: Thank them for their precious time and share the good their products are doing in the lives of patients. Ask key questions regarding the world needing inspirational leaders; share key outcomes for the day; have them up sharing their key learnings.

N NAVIGATE CONTENT	Teach: NOTE: The one who is doing the teaching is doing the learning.	1) Have participants teach four stages of development in team; 2) practice skill diagnosis with a variety of mini case studies; 3) have participants write their own stories going through the four development levels; 4) utilizing a card sort, sort the behaviors from four development levels and four leadership styles. Remember: Activities always move • from easy to difficult • from individual to group.	• Visual • Auditory • Kinesthetic
	REVIEW— The more the review, the deeper the neural connections	SLII Game, Diagnosis + Practice doing all four leadership styles with observer and checklist (out of context)	

G GENERATE MEANING	Move to long-term memory	Flip chart activity: 1) What have you learned so far that you want to remember? 2) What would the benefits of using or applying your learning be for (in three columns) you, others, and your organization?
A APPLY TO REAL WORLD	Demonstrate new skills NOTE: Help people be smart in the way they *are* smart.	• Articulate critical tasks their direct reports need to do. • Have people create job aids by saying what a D1, D2, D3, and D4 would look like on those tasks or goals. • Teams determine what an S1, S2, S3, and S4 look like on those tasks or goals. • Team analysis and diagnosing team activity—participants fill out worksheets on a team analysis grid, diagnosing direct reports on critical tasks or goals. • Partnering for performance meeting with one direct report; team debrief.

G GAUGE AND CELEBRATE	Look how much was learned!	Crossword puzzle or game debrief of knowledge- and comprehension-level questions; group mind map of key learnings of the day; write the five visible signs people will see them doing differently as a result of this training.
E EXTEND LEARNING TO ACTION	Support to act on best intentions	Email tips; follow-up podcasts from senior leaders who have captured success stories and shared key business results being impacted by use of the Situational Leadership® II language with direct reports.

In designing this training, we followed the three 70/30 principles:

1. Learners do 70 percent of the talking and 30 percent of the listening.

2. Teachers dedicate 70 percent of their preparation to "how" (learning design) and 30 percent to "what" (content) they will teach.

3. Learners practice 70 percent of the time.

Creating multiple touch points and teaching content critical to helping individuals achieve organizational goals results in individuals becoming powerful learners who feel important. As you design your workshop and build a culture of learning through optimal design, remember that people want to be magnificent. They want to be smart. And it's up to us to make sure we create opportunities for that to happen.

 Fuel Up: Chapter Exercise: Course Look and Feel

Take time during the development phase to determine the look and feel of your training program. Putting thought into the visual design of the project will help with the perception of quality and professionalism. Use the Visual Language section of this chapter to help.

Fill in the following mind map to begin the visual conversation. Fill out your associations to each circle's topic—for example, "What emotions do I want to elicit with the visuals in my class?"

⛽ Fuel Up: Chapter Exercise: Materials Review Checklist

Use this chart to do a pre-launch review of your web-based training (WBT) or technology-supported learning, presentations, and printed documents.

Materials Review Checklist

	WBT / Tech. Learning Considerations	Presentations	Printed Docs	NOTES
Big Ideas:				
Learner Relevance				
Alignment to Business Goals				
One Idea per Page				
Structure / Flow				
Expected Outcomes				
Grammar / Spelling:				
Spell-Checker				
Grammar-Checker				
Data Are Visual / Easy to Read				
Text Is Clear, Direct				
Humor Is Appropriate				
Text / Images Fit on Page				
Proper Nouns Are Correct				
Screenshots Are Correct				
Online Learning:				
Interface Is Intuitive		N/A	N/A	
Buttons / Links Work			N/A	
Graphics Support Content				
Help Is Available and Useful				

IMPLEMENTATION

Tell me and I forget. Teach me and I remember.
Involve me and I learn.

- Benjamin Franklin

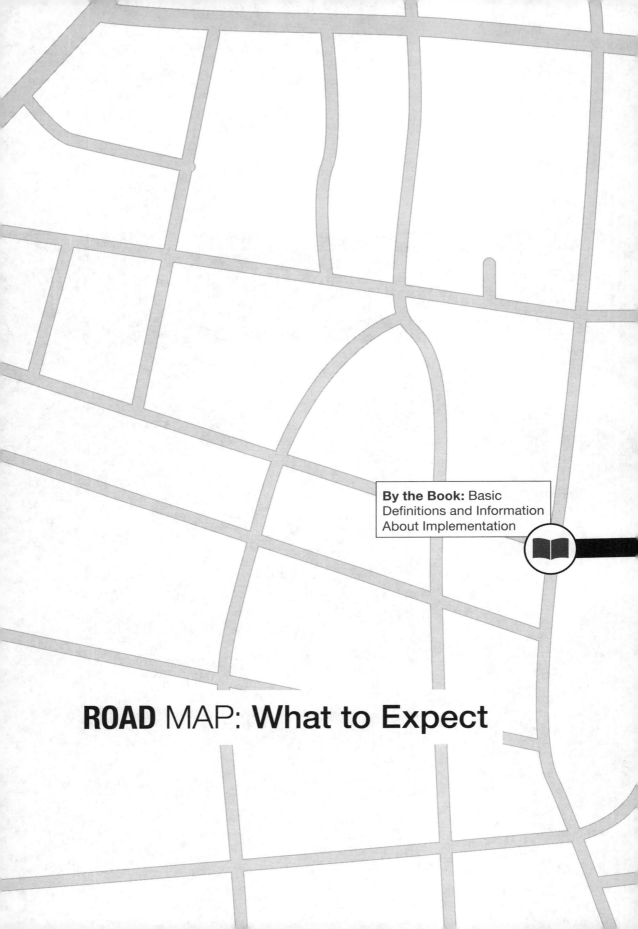

By the Book: Basic Definitions and Information About Implementation

ROAD MAP: What to Expect

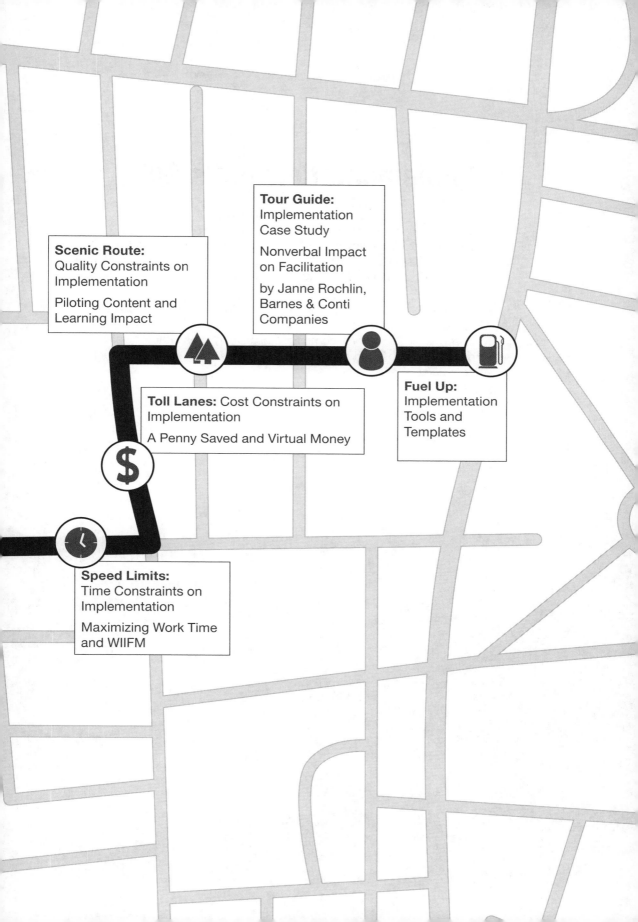

Scenic Route:
Quality Constraints on Implementation

Piloting Content and Learning Impact

Tour Guide:
Implementation Case Study

Nonverbal Impact on Facilitation

by Janne Rochlin, Barnes & Conti Companies

Toll Lanes: Cost Constraints on Implementation

A Penny Saved and Virtual Money

Fuel Up:
Implementation Tools and Templates

Speed Limits:
Time Constraints on Implementation

Maximizing Work Time and WIIFM

Implementation: Let's Go!

All that work, and you're finally ready to leave for your training journey. It might seem as though the training is on autopilot and you can sit back and enjoy the experience, but that isn't the case. In fact, there are several aspects that can still be taken into account to save time, reduce cost, or increase quality.

Just like the moment when you can finally start your road trip, this stage of the journey can be the most exciting part. You finally get to see all of your efforts come together. During this chapter we will discuss how to avoid problems and mitigate risk points within each constraint.

📖 By the Book: Implementation

Implementation is the most visible part of the training project. For many learning and development (L&D) professionals, this is the point at which natural strengths and the desire to facilitate come out. However, it is really important to be mindful of the training project's goals throughout the entire event.

Key Considerations:

- Preparation
    - ▸ Facilitator(s)
    - ▸ Materials
    - ▸ Location
- Execution
    - ▸ Follow the script—stay away from improvisation
    - ▸ Remember to always link to the WIIFM
    - ▸ Get feedback as you go
- Flawless Delivery
    - ▸ Results from preparation and execution

The name of the implementation game is preparation. Skilled facilitators have a tendency to "wing it" and go off script. Facilitators (who are not also designers) may have preferred activities that they want to add in, but they don't actually align with the objectives. Remember, all of the work leading up to this point was for a reason—to strategically link learning to results. Changing the training while in progress derails a lot of effort—and there is no bigger waste of time or money than that.

⏱ Speed Limits: Time Constraints

In the case of implementation, the largest time constraint usually encountered is that of taking people out of their jobs. If you are going to ask people to leave their work for an hour, a day, or even longer for your training event, you have to make sure the time is well spent.

1. Maximizing Work Time—To shrink required time away from the job, assign constructive pre-work before class. Have participants come to the class (in-person or through a virtual meeting) with any rote or basic knowledge.

    a. Knowledge First, Skills During, Application After

2. WIIFM—The best way to ensure that participants feel that their time was spent on valuable information is to frequently and consistently align content with the participants' motivation factors.

    a. Goals Lists and Participant-Directed Learning

    b. Techniques for Creating Aha Moments

Maximizing Work Time—Knowledge First, Skills During, Application After

Here's a formula that works for making sure that time spent out of the job is as valuable as possible.

(Knowledge = Pre-work)

Assign pre-work to take care of the knowledge pieces of the learning material. New knowledge (vocabulary, policy, diagrams) is easily acquired outside of the classroom.

(Skills = Classwork)

This leaves class time (in-person or virtual) for learning and practicing skills and higher-level learning. Use peers and facilitators for feedback and deeper understanding.

(Application = Follow-up)

Reinforce learning after the event. Most of the learner's ability to retain learning and change behavior comes after training. Don't lose the chance to create results.

WIIFM—Goals Lists and Participant-Directed Learning

What I want to know is…What's in it for me? WIIFM?

Great question! We have already discussed some of the skills you will learn from this session. Why don't we talk about what you want to get out of the class?

Well, I guess I really need to learn this new software, which you said was an objective. But I also need to know when to use it.

Sounds like a good goal. Let's write that down along with any other goals you have on your flip chart. Whenever you feel that we've addressed your goal, check it off.

OK. And if I still haven't hit some of my goals by the end of the training?

We will make a plan for following up, and I will refer you to other resources that can help. This class is about you!

WIIFM—Techniques for Creating Aha Moments

During the greatest speeches of all time, there is a moment of revelation—a point at which the audience collectively gasps in amazement. These "lightbulb" or "aha" moments should happen in training as well. Here are the instructions for building an "aha" moment for learners.

Aha Moments:

a. Identify your spark for change. Great learning comes down to a change in behavior—clearly understand what change you are asking your learners to make.

b. Build a safe foundation. Creating a shift in thinking is only likely to happen if you have engineered a comfortable and safe environment.

c. Make your case for change by bridging ideas. Guide learners to the change.

d. Illuminate the vision. Help your learners see how the future is brighter because they will be utilizing their new skills.

$ Toll Lanes: Cost Constraints

Training space, travel, food, materials, workbooks—the costs of a classroom training event add up quickly. Even training through a live virtual meeting can come with some serious price tags for shipping materials or software licenses. Keeping costs as low as possible means focusing on the highest value-add items, and being prepared to think on your feet.

1. A Penny Saved—Keeping costs low for classroom training events.

   a. Location, Location, Location

   b. Breaks as Learning Opportunities

2. Virtual Money—A few ideas for saving money with online learning events.

   a. Big Value Activities

A Penny Saved—Location, Location, Location

If saving money is your goal, there are ways to cut costs at any training location through direct savings, leveraging existing resources, and minimizing time away from the job.

Classroom (On Job Site)

1. Ask learners to bring their own lunch, or break for lunch and let learners seek out lunch options on their own rather than providing it.

2. Have learners bring their own laptops as necessary.

3. Include local subject matter experts to help facilitate. (Volunteer as stretch assignment.)

4. Schedule a session so that it has minimal impact on productivity.

5. Share physical resources with other departments—split costs.

Meeting Space (Off Job Site)

1. Forego heavy participant guides (use blank notebooks).

2. Go with the cheaper sandwich option for lunch.

3. Pick up granola bars or candy from a bulk store rather than paying a caterer for afternoon snacks.

4. Don't pay for location upgrades such as wireless Internet unless you really need it.

5. Consider dropping your presentation slides. You can skip the cost of renting or shipping a projector and include any necessary visuals in a workbook or handout.

6. Build relationships with locally owned businesses.

A Penny Saved—Breaks as Learning Opportunities

You will want to squeeze every bit of value out of the time your participants spend with you. Here are some tips for leveraging "downtime" while still giving learners the breaks they need.

Parking Lot

- After introductions, but before class really begins, introduce the "parking lot" where participants can write questions that they would like answered.

- Before each break, encourage participants to add questions as needed, and if their question has been addressed, cross it out on the flip chart.

Gallery Walk

- Post multiple flip charts around the room, each with a different class topic or content question written on it.

- Instruct participants to add their thoughts during breaks or lunch.

Action Planning

- During each break, have participants choose a learning partner and share the one or two top things they learned from the previous content. Then, have them commit to one action item and write it in their notebooks.

Personal Learning Objectives

- In the participant guides, provide a page on learning objectives. In addition to the stated objectives of the class, include space for participants to write.

- Before the start of a content section, have participants write down the WIIFM for that section next to the learning objectives.

- During breaks, instruct learners to review their WIIFM notes and ask questions.

Virtual Money—Big-Value Activities

Increase the effectiveness of self-paced online learning as well as synchronous (virtual) learning events and make sure that learners are getting the most out of their screen time. Avoid busywork—instead opt for experiences that engage!

Make interfaces easy to understand, and clearly outline objectives for learners.

Provide helpful resources in the form of search boxes and FAQs.

Drag-and-drop does not equal interactivity. Think, "Is this a meaningful learning experience?" Interfaces and simulations should mirror the real world as much as possible.

Include access for mobile devices when possible.

"Gamification" is the new "feedback." Add scores and badges to asynchronous learning to help with engagement. For repeat use, post a high-score board on your intranet. This helps with all methods of learning!

⚑ Scenic Route: Quality or Scope Constraints

The facilitator (whether or not this is also the designer) can control the execution of the event and provide feedback to the design team. Most of all, a prepared and knowledgeable facilitator can incorporate several techniques to promote learning transfer.

1. Piloting Content—Test everything! When quality counts, don't let anything get implemented without a thorough vetting.

   a. Conducting Pilot Classes

2. Learning Impact—The two biggest influences on learning transfer.

   a. Facilitator Preparation

   b. Ways to Promote Behavior Change

Piloting Content—Conducting Pilot Classes

The military would never purchase new jets and planes without having an experienced pilot test them. Similarly, you shouldn't even think of implementing a widescale training without holding a pilot training class ahead of your launch date. Consider the following tactics for holding a pilot class.

	Invite a mix of attendees: SMEs, stakeholders, target learners.
	Tell them it's a pilot—they will be excited to be a part of it.
	Before the class begins, explain the purpose of the class.
	Set expectations for the class—without apologizing for bumps.
	Make participants feel like a part of the project—not lab rats.
	Instruct participants to hold feedback until after the class.
	Include at least one independent observer with a checklist.
	Prepare the facilitator for a bumpy delivery.
	Ask for written feedback (level 1 evaluation) and hold a verbal session.
	Send thank-you cards to participants within a week of the pilot.

Learning Impact—Facilitator Preparation

For classroom training, facilitation is absolutely key. A stellar facilitator can take a class from "meh" to "wow" and from low energy to high energy. A poor facilitator can make outstanding training classes totally worthless. While becoming a stellar facilitator takes practice and a good skill set, it is safe to say that you won't get there without adequate preparation.

 Spend lots of time ahead practicing the facilitation. There is no hard-and-fast rule for how much time is needed. Practice as many times as it takes to feel natural with the content.

 Understand how to take the pulse of the room and intervene. When energy is low, be prepared to take a break, or introduce an energizing activity.

 Cure the disease, not the symptoms. Facilitators should review the analysis results to understand the purpose of the class from a strategic perspective.

 Use your resources. If there is technical content that you don't feel comfortable with, find a credible expert to help with the facilitation.

 Prepare for scrapes and bruises along the way. Proactively assess and mitigate risks, such as forgetting your slides, or technology issues. Take part in design meetings throughout the project to understand the alignment with company goals.

 Remember, you are the catalyst for change. As the facilitator you need to be able to explain to learners why they are here, and the WIIFM behind the class. Be prepared for skeptics.

Learning Impact—Ways to Promote Behavior Change

When it comes down to the bottom line, the training class only exists to improve and increase on-the-job performance, to create a change in behaviors that will benefit the employee and the employer.

During implementation, the facilitator and anyone else supporting the training event should do everything they can to promote that behavior change.

Be Flexible and Debrief Well:

Adjust timing and activities as needed to meet the learning objectives of the class. If you have a clear vision of the outcomes of the class, you shouldn't get too far off of the plan.

Manage Expectations:

It's important for learners to understand their role in the classroom. The facilitator can't make magic happen—he or she can help the learners take charge of their own transformation. If appropriate, try explaining some adult learning principles so that learners understand the process better.

Spend Time Clearing the Air:

If the training is in the middle of a big change, encourage discussion as a large group or in partners about how the change affects learners. Unless participants can process their concerns, they will never be able to change their behavior.

Address Systemic Issues:

If technological, supervisory, environmental, or policy issues are going to prevent learners from using their new skills on the job, discuss them in the classroom and escalate the issue to change makers in your organization.

⑧ Tour Guide: Nonverbal Impact on Facilitation

Janne Rochlin, Barnes & Conti Companies

In my work as a facilitator of leadership and interpersonal communication skills, I emphasize the nonverbal impact of communication: matching the visuals to the words so that my message is received in the manner it is intended. To that end, I encourage other facilitators to have a conversation with a client to find out how the participants in a training session will be dressed so that the facilitator can match the look of the participants. That way, the participants will not be distracted by the appearance of the facilitator and will make judgments of the facilitator based not on appearance but on the intended message.

In a particular instance, I violated my own expectations.

We had a biotech client based in Silicon Valley. At the home office resided the research and development (R&D) department and the business units. Manufacturing was done in the Midwest. In the work that we did at corporate headquarters, business-casual dress was the standard, much as it was for most of our clients. I was asked to design a week-long program at the plant in a small Midwestern city that would include leadership skills training, influence skills training, and individual consulting and coaching using a personal type instrument.

I arrived on Monday morning in the early spring wearing my best business casual: trousers, a blouse, and, for good measure, a lovely spring jacket. The first person to arrive was the plant manager. He was wearing jeans and a polo shirt. No bells went off. As the rest of the participants filtered in, I knew I was in trouble. Overalls, work jumpers, industrial boots, and baseball caps with various sayings and teams printed on them including one with fake seagull droppings. They had been told that the sessions were mandatory, and some of them had worked the graveyard shift before coming to the class.

135

Before I even began the introduction, I could feel the hostility and mistrust emanating from the participants. I could just imagine the thoughts going through their heads: "She's from the home office, and she's here to help us." I knew no one was hearing the intended message that morning.

At lunch, I returned to my hotel and changed into jeans and a T-shirt. When the afternoon resumed, I disclosed that I had made a mistake and that I was there not to "fix" them but to help them to build the skills that would further their ability to contribute to the organization. I asked for a tour of the plant in full manufacturing dress: overalls, work boots, and hard hat.

By the third day, I was invited to a community baseball game to meet the families and out for pizza and beer with the participants. The one-on-one coaching sessions were done on their turf, in the plant, and I made sure to mirror the energy of the individual participants during those sessions.

If I had ever doubted the power of nonverbal communication and the messages we send with our visuals, this experience cemented my belief.

🅿️ Fuel Up: Chapter Exercise: Designing a Follow-Up Activity

Increase your impact by designing a reinforcement activity for your class. Use this chapter as guidance for how to ensure learning transfer.

1. What behavior is likely to go unused back on the job?

2. Why is this behavior at risk from becoming a permanent performance change? (List retention and systemic reasons.)

3. Identify specific ways follow-up or reinforcement will help with the behavior change.

4. Use the space below to create a plan for the follow-up activity. Don't forget about how you will support it logistically.

🔋 Fuel Up: Chapter Tool: Facilitator Preparation Checklist

Here is a checklist to help a facilitator prepare for a classroom-training event.

- ☐ Can you clearly and simply state the goals of the class?

- ☐ Do you feel comfortable facilitating all of the content?

- ☐ Have you practiced each part so that you do not need to read from your facilitator's guide?

- ☐ Can you tell your own stories with the content? You need to be able to illustrate examples with stories that are authentic to you.

- ☐ At what points of the class do you expect energy to be low? How will you bring it back up?

- ☐ What are the risk points with the class content from an organizational, emotional, and engagement standpoint? Do you have a plan for responding to these issues?

- ☐ What are the risk points with the class from an environmental and a technological standpoint? What is your back-up plan?

- ☐ Are the guest speakers prepared for their parts? Are they aware of the dates and times that they are expected?

- ☐ Have your learners been provided with pre-work and expectations for the class?

- ☐ Have all materials (workbooks, flip charts, speakers, projector, and so forth) been delivered to the event?

- ☐ Is the classroom set up and clean?

- ☐ Have you tested all technology on the same day as the training?

Make sure you have water and are wearing clothing that you feel confident in. Turn your mobile phone off or on vibrate. Greet learners as they come in and mingle with them while people are getting settled.

EVALUATION

In the end, you're measured not by how much you undertake but by what you finally accomplish.

- Donald Trump

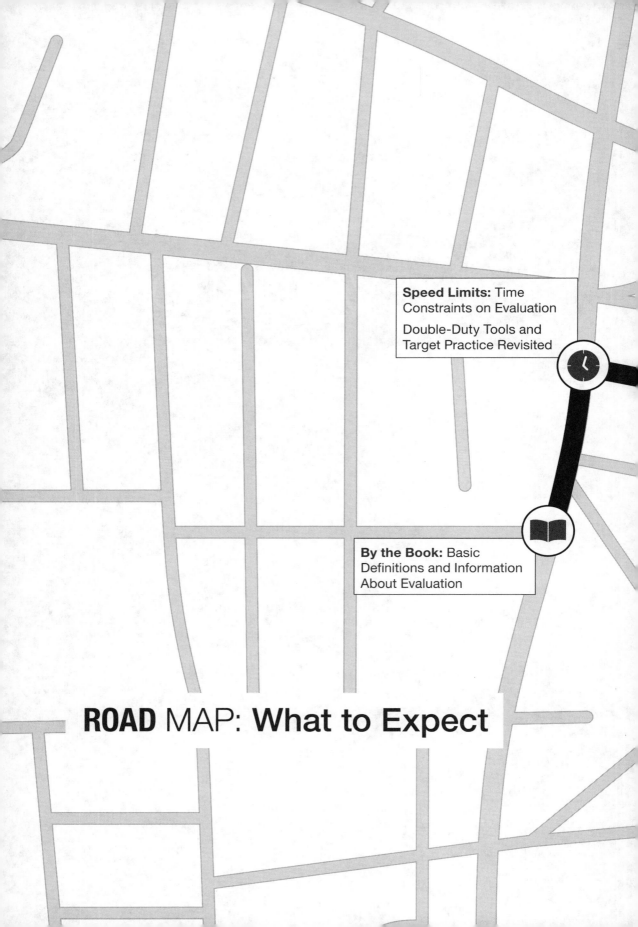

Speed Limits: Time Constraints on Evaluation

Double-Duty Tools and Target Practice Revisited

By the Book: Basic Definitions and Information About Evaluation

ROAD MAP: What to Expect

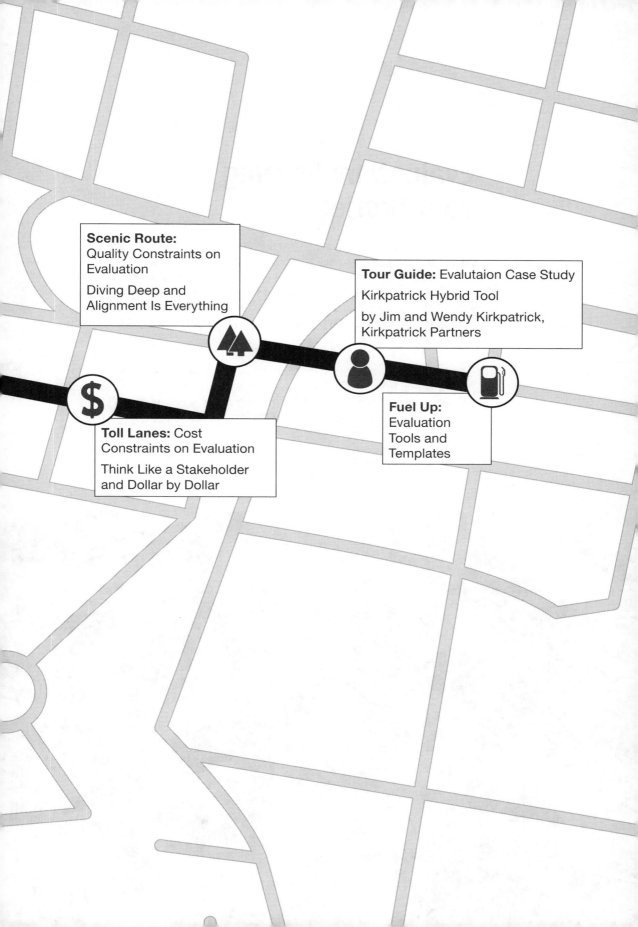

Evaluation: Sharing Your Stories

After a great trip, you usually have some good memories to look back on. Hopefully, you also have some photos to show your friends and entertaining tales for your next party. Your journey may have been amazing and life-changing, but to share your experiences, you need to have some kind of proof. If you took pictures and collected souvenirs throughout the trip, your friends and family will get to see just how great it was.

The training design step of evaluation works the same way as photographs from a vacation. As a designer, you need to be able to show the impact and value of the training project, and you can't wait until the end of the project to begin thinking about it.

The output of the evaluation phase is a four-part deliverable telling the story of the training project's impact on your organization.

144

By the Book: Evaluation

Evaluation is the step of the instructional systems design (ISD) process that improves programs, drives on-the-job application and measures impact of a training project. Measures can be qualitative (testimonials, anecdotes, and so forth) or quantitative (financial metrics, productivity statistics, and so forth).

Evaluation planning should be done at the beginning of the project so that data can be gathered throughout the process, not just at the end. The degree to which a program is ultimately successful, and that success is defendable, is enhanced by starting with the end in mind. That allows for targeted training, reinforcement, and evaluation that all lead to the ultimate measures of success.

Key Considerations:

- Create an evaluation plan after completing your analysis.
- Align your metrics to the goals of your organization and project.
- Evaluation is a part of the entire ISD process—not a step at the end.
- Determine what matters to your stakeholders and tell that story.

The most important value of the evaluation step is to tell the success story of your training project to stakeholders.

The traditional model for evaluating training program impact was developed by Dr. Don Kirkpatrick in the 1950s and consists of four levels: reaction, learning, behavior, and results. The graphic below is an adaptation of the four levels chart.

Training Event

Program Design — Increase effort and resources		Evaluation Design — Increase effort and resources
Satisfaction and Expectations	Reaction	
Knowledge and Skills	Learning	
Performance Change	Behavior	
Business Impact	Results	

Level	Description	Sample Metrics	Important Information
1: Reaction	How well do participants react to the training?	1–5 Survey Questions, "Plus / Deltas," "Start / Stop / Continue"	Identify participant expectations and obstacles.
2: Learning	How well do participants meet objectives; gain new knowledge, skills, or attitudes?	Written / Verbal Tests Action Plans Role-Play w/ Observer Demonstrate Skills	This piece of the puzzle determines if learners can do what you wanted them to do.
3: Behavior	To what degree do participants take learning and use it to change behavior on the job?	Direct Observations Action Plan Monitoring Supervisor Interviews Surveys	If participants achieved learning, but did not change behavior, systemic issues are present.
4: Results	What results are seen as a result of the behavior change from the training event?	Productivity Numbers Increase in Revenue Decrease in Errors Higher Retention Higher Engagement	**This is the information your stakeholders care about!**

⏱ Speed Limits: Time Constraints

The tendency to plan and execute the evaluation of a training project after the event itself has led to the perception that it takes a large amount of time. Because the event has already taken place, many stakeholders may be hesitant to "buy in" to an extended timeline for evaluation. These tools will help you incorporate evaluation throughout your project, and measure your impact.

1. Double Duty—Use the fewest tools to measure the aspects of greatest impact to your training project.

    a. Levels 1 and 2

    b. Levels 2 and 3

2. Target Practice Revisited—Just as in the analysis phase, shooting scattershot with your evaluation will return piles of irrelevant data to sort through. Be focused in your approach to save time.

    a. Fresh Data

    b. Knowing What to Look For

Double Duty—Levels 1 and 2

Beyond using templates for your evaluation tools, the best way to save yourself time is to make your tools work twice as hard for you. One of these "double-duty" methods is to combine your level 1 and level 2 tools. Leverage the end-of-training survey you usually send out to record objective completion.

This level 1/level 2 tool should direct the learner toward the ultimate purpose of the program; which is to improve their performance (level 3), in order to make a contribution to the mission or goals of the organization (L4). This can simply be done by adding questions that ask participants to think of how they will apply their new skills, or describe the success they will see as a result of their efforts.

Typical Learner Questions:

Name (Required)
Position / Team / Tenure in Role: (As Needed for Relevant Data)
Contact Info: (As Needed If Not on Record)

Level 1 questions are learner centered, use a rating scale (not pictured), and provide space for additional notes.	Level 1 Reaction Questions:
	1. I was able to relate the knowledge and skills of this class to my job.
	2. I felt engaged and included by the facilitator.
	3. I feel that my expectations of the class were met.
	4. The experiences and style of the facilitator helped cause the success of my learning experience.
	5. I am confident in my ability to practice my new skills on the job.
These example level 2s use reflective questions to help learners think about what they have learned and how they will apply it. You can also use straight-forward	Level 2 Learning Questions:
	6. What are the first steps you will take to use your new skills on the job?
	7. Which learning objective will have the largest impact on your work? Why?
	8. What did you learn from XYZ activity that will affect how you will do your job?
	9. What feedback did you get from the role-play activity? Will the feedback change how you apply your new skills?
	10. Use the action planning tool (provided) to map out how and when you will use your new skills in the next three weeks.

Double Duty—Levels 2 and 3

The difference between level 2 and level 3 is that the performance is measured in the classroom for the learning level and on the job for the behavior level. In most cases, though, the performance being measured should be the same for both levels.

Using a double-duty level 2 and 3 evaluation saves time not only when creating the tools, but also when analyzing your results. Here are some examples.

Example 1:	Level 2 Tool: Action Plan	Some Results:
Managers in a "Holding Difficult Conversations" workshop	**Level 3 Change:** Reflection/ Success of Action Plan	Many participants created specific and tactical action plans, and used their plans as job aids during follow-up meetings.

Example 2:	Level 2 Tool: Role-Play in Class With Observer Feedback Form	Some Results:
Customer service managers with the objective of selling a premium package to new customers.	**Level 3 Change:** Same Feedback Form Utilized by Manager During Actual Call	High scores from the classroom observation dropped lower for level 3. A diagnosis showed that reinforcement of the package details was needed. A follow-up refresher was added, and scores improved.

Target Practice Revisited—Fresh Data

Just like with the analysis phase, evaluation methods should be focused clearly on specific metrics. If time is a constraint, it doesn't pay to use a large net. Instead target the data that will return the most relevant and important information.

Immediacy is a key aspect to the value data can have. Think about a typical leadership development course in which high potential is preparing for a leadership role. The level 2 (learning) and level 3 (behavior) data for the participants are critical to senior leaders, who will be looking for their next promotion within a few months.

Collecting data—and then letting those data sit untouched—is a waste. It uses up time spent preparing the evaluation and conducting it without actually being able to use the data. It also erodes your credibility, and makes your participants less likely to participate in evaluation in the future.

Always include time in your project plan for analyzing your evaluation data!

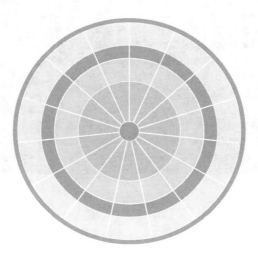

Target Practice Revisited—Knowing What to Look For

One of the most difficult skills to acquire is that of interpreting data. If level 1 surveys come back and show a general dissatisfaction with the training event, you need to know how to dig into the root cause of the issue and how to take action.

1. Perform the Sniff Test Again—Make sure you vet each of your questions before you begin using evaluation tools.

2. Provide Space for Why—Likert scales (number ratings) are easiest to compute, but allowing space for participants to include their rationale may be helpful.

3. Think Systemically—Be sure to evaluate root cause issues, not their symptoms.

4. Don't Jump to Conclusions—Poor ratings on a level 1 evaluation could indicate a need to better level-set expectations rather than a comment on the value of the class.

5. Correlation, Not Causation—If participants score very well each year in November and December, don't assume that you need to hold classes only in winter. The problem might be that September and October participants are under tight deadlines because of the fiscal year end.

6. Be Proactive—Some people are worried about evaluating because it might return "bad" numbers when the stakeholder isn't even asking for an evaluation. Think about it—wouldn't you rather know that there are things to fix before you have to show up at a board meeting?

⑤ Toll Lanes: Cost Constraints

The number-one reason that evaluations are shut down before they can begin is the inability of learning and development (L&D) professionals to justify the cost. Ironically, during tough times, training suffers from not having the metrics to prove its own value. Conducting an evaluation is critical for current training projects—as well as conversations with stakeholders down the road.

1. Think Like a Stakeholder—What does it take for you to open your wallet? Imagine what your clients want to hear, and make sure you evaluate it!

   a. Learner-Centered Metrics

   b. Tell a Qualitative and Quantitative Story

2. Dollar by Dollar—A comparison of evaluation tools and their relative costs.

   a. More About Formative Evaluation

Think Like a Stakeholder—Learner-Centered Metrics

Your learners are stakeholders or clients too. Getting the most honest and objective measures from participants is key to having valid measurement of training impact. One way to increase the value of learner input is to change our evaluation tools to a learner-centered, rather than training-centered, approach.

Here's the idea: Stop framing questions like "Rate the effectiveness of the facilitator." Instead, create a first-person question set, as in "My learning experience was helped by the effectiveness of the facilitator."

Want more?

Facilitator-centered	▶	Learner-centered
The class provided the tools and skills to do better on the job.	▶	I feel equipped to do my job better as a result of this training.
The facilitator was knowledgeable and credible.	▶	I was able to get answers to all of my questions on this topic.
The objectives of the class were clearly stated.	▶	I understood the objectives of the class.
The class content is relevant and important.	▶	I feel that the training is relevant to my current role.

Think Like a Stakeholder—Tell a Qualitative and Quantitative Story

Ultimately evaluating a training program isn't just about showing the impact of that class; it's also about justifying the cost of creating it. Whether you measure ROI (return on investment) or ROE (return on effort), telling the story of the training's success is critical.

First, you need to have some idea of what your stakeholders want to hear. Will they respond to data, or will qualitative information be more impactful? If you aren't sure, it's smart to include both kinds of information.

Here are some examples of both quantitative and qualitative data

Quantitative	Qualitative
Number of learners reached	Testimonials by participants
Cost of training event	Anecdotes about customer service
Decrease in attrition	
	Success stories using new KSAs
Increase in sales	
Increase in customer satisfaction %	Additional client opportunities
	Employee engagement stories

Second, make sure you speak strategically. If you did your analysis properly, then you already know which business goals and initiatives you are aligned with, and those are the things your stakeholders will most likely care about.

Here is one example of how you might present your story to your stakeholders.

4 RESULTS	Start with the results. Did you affect the goal or initiative that you set out to achieve? The first message: "We hit our goal. Let me tell you how."
1 EXPECTATIONS	We made sure that the training participants found it relevant and that they understood the connection between the training and their job. Over 77 percent of our learners believe that this training will help them hit their annual productivity goals.
2 LEARNING	Participants were evaluated to make sure that they acquired the skills needed to affect our business goals. More than half of the learners scored perfectly across the board, and everyone scored over 85 percent. Two senior leaders in the class told us that this training changed how they will conduct their business meetings in the future.
3 BEHAVIOR	Learners were re-evaluated back on the job after three months. Their job performance scores were slightly lower than the training scores. Only 33 percent received perfect scores from their supervisor's observation, while many others dropped below 85 percent. The slight decrease indicated a systemic issue other than training— such as technology, process, or management. We were able to diagnose the issue quickly and improve scores.
4 RESULTS	Because of these efforts, the training project was a success. Employees were able to get up to speed quickly with their new skills and had one and half times their previous productivity numbers. Our revenue has increased by 26 percent since the first training event a year ago. Customer satisfaction numbers are also higher. We have exceeded the goals of the project, on time and on budget.

Dollar by Dollar—More About Formative Evaluation

In an ideal world without budgets or timelines, each data point in an evaluation would be triangulated (verified by three different types of measurement), and each tool would be objective, valid, and reliable.

Unfortunately, when the budget is scarce, it can be very difficult to justify a thorough evaluation. I have had a good many stakeholders wave off the evaluation as unnecessary. However, as the person responsible for creating a high-value product on budget, this is required information. Sometimes, my compromise is to do a less formal (formative) evaluation using the facilitator or a third-party observer.

Facilitator	Observer
• Keep a "parking lot" or other communal space for logging unaddressed questions (level 1 or 2).	• Keep an accurate timetable and compare it to expected time spent on activities. Note why there are significant differences.
• Take note of group discussions that veer off course or take longer than expected (level 1 or 2).	• Document energy and participation levels throughout event (very subjective).
• Document questions asked during the event (level 2).	• During breaks wander between participants and ask for a "temperature check."
• Periodically review training objectives and ask participants if they feel comfortable with each one covered so far (level 2).	• Conduct a "Plus/Delta" conversation at the end of the event. Ask participants to give thoughts on strong points about the training as well as things that should change.
• Use teach-backs and role-play and take note of trends of undeveloped or incorrect behavior (level 2).	• Ask participants what obstacles they expect back on the job that would prevent them from utilizing their new knowledge or skills (level 1).
• Conduct a "Start/Stop/Continue." Ask participants to write down at least one thing that needs to be added to the training, one thing that should be removed, and one strong point that should continue (level 1).	

157

⬙ Scenic Route: Quality or Scope Constraints

If quality is the largest constraint for your training project, then the evaluation stage is your proving ground. To show the evidence of a high-quality impact, use evaluation measures wisely.

1. Diving Deep on Learning and Behavior—Specifics on gauging learning effectiveness and behavior change.

    a. Level 2 Breakdown

    b. Level 3 Breakdown

2. Alignment Is Everything—Know which results are the most crucial to the organization and make sure your training is in alignment.

    a. Leading Indicators

    b. Vision and Mission in Training

Diving Deep—Level 2 Learning Breakdown

How do you evaluate learning besides tests? Here are a few examples based on levels of learning. Please note that the "evaluation" stage here references Bloom's taxonomy and not the step of the ADDIE model.

What's Bloom's taxonomy? Check it out here.

Knowledge:	• Write questions • Oral exam • Label diagrams • Recalls a model
Comprehension:	• Uses open-ended questions • Explains a task • Uses job aids • Sorts cards
Application:	• Demonstrates tool • Follows instructions • Solves a new problem using knowledge
Analysis:	• Troubleshoots a problem • Explains the "why" of a question • Diagrams and explains a model • Can train others on knowledge and skills
Synthesis:	• Relates knowledge to their job • Creates new content or process based on skills • Defends a position with credibility • Critiques a strategy or position based on expertise
Evaluation:	• Predict outcomes based on expertise • Select a strategy and defend the choice • Compares different solutions and explains the best one • Overcomes obstacles and problems while using skill

Diving Deep—Level 3 Behavior Breakdown

There are a multitude of ways to measure performance on the job. Most correlate well to a level 2 evaluation (see double-duty tools) to save time and money. Remember that measuring level 3 is critical to being able to tell a success story. If you don't know how your learners performed on the job, you have no idea if your training was impactful.

Retained Knowledge:
- List or recall items verbally
- Labels diagram or model
- Explain tasks
- Uses job aids

Uses Skills:
- Demonstrates problem solving
- Explains "why" of process
- Observed completing tasks
- Consistently meets goals

Shows Competency:
- Creates new solutions
- Regarded as an "expert"
- Teaches others
- Exceeds performance goals

Alignment Is Everything—Leading Indicators

Earlier in this chapter, we discussed combining your evaluation tools to save time during the evaluation of your training project. To increase quality, and get results faster, consider combining levels 3 and 4 into a hybrid tool.

Essentially, the level 3 and 4 hybrid combines an assessment of on-the-job behaviors (level 3) with leading indicators (level 4) to see early signs of the impact of your training project.

Think of the results you want from the project as the final destination, but the trip to get there could take quite a while. The passengers in your car are antsy and keep asking, "Are we there yet?" (Just like stakeholders!) So, you say, "We aren't in Key West yet, but we got theme park tickets for Orlando, so we're stopping there on the way!" In other words, "Our retention numbers won't reflect the impact of this program for over a year, but our level 3 and 4 hybrid results give us some indication that we are moving the needle in the right direction!"

For more on the New Four Levels, check out the resources and workshops provided by the Kirkpatrick Partners

Using this method helps your stakeholders, and learners, get a sense of progress as the impact is happening. The power is in identifying the leading indicators. These are measurements you can take—like taking a pulse—during the level 3 evaluation that indicates points of success or failure.

Examples:

1. To what degree are you applying what you learned? (Provide a list of behaviors and skills.)

2. What has contributed to your success on XYZ initiative?

3. What are the barriers to success in applying your new skills?

4. What results are you seeing from applying your new skills?

5. How do you know you have been successful?

Put the power of feedback in the hands of your learners!

Alignment Is Everything—Vision and Mission in Training

Demonstrating the alignment among individual employee goals, project goals, and organizational goals (vision or mission) is critical both for your stakeholders and your participants. An easy way to demonstrate this is through an impact map. The impact map demonstrates to your participants why the time they spent in training directly impacts not only their jobs, but the organization as well. This is key in increasing participation and employee engagement.

The impact map builds on the tools from earlier chapters. If you complete the alignment exercises along the way, most of this content will already be built!

Vision	What is the organization's stated vision? A vision is the view of what the future looks like.
Mission	What is the organization's stated mission? A mission is how the organization goes about achieving the vision of the future.
Goals	What important organizational initiative or goal did the training focus on that helps the organization work toward its mission?
Evaluation Results	What is the success story? What are the results that show how behavior, learning, and expectations moved the organization toward its goals?

👤 Tour Guide: Kirkpatrick Hybrid Tool

Kirkpatrick Partners, LLC

For Delayed Use After Training

Instructions: This template includes a variety of sample questions for each dimension of levels appropriate for evaluating outcomes some time after the training has taken place. Select a few questions from each dimension (for example, on-the-job behavior, drivers, etc.) that will provide the data you need to make good decisions, and create a chain of evidence for the business value of your training initiative.

Timing: Post-training event, after the drivers are engaged, and enough time passes for participants to apply the new skills on the job. The timing will vary depending upon the type of knowledge or skills being taught.

Format: Survey, interview, or focus group

Rating Scale: Choose one of the following for rating scale questions:

1=Strongly Disagree	2=Disagree	3=Agree	4=Strongly Agree

Strongly Disagree								Strongly Agree	
1	2	3	4	5	6	7	8	9	10

Tip: To get the richest possible data, provide a comment field for as many questions as possible. Keep in mind the time and resources required to tabulate handwritten responces.

Delayed Level 1: Reaction

Relevance

Rating Scale Questions

- This course provided all of the information I needed to be able to perform the skills taught on the job.

- The information provided in this course is fully applicable to my job.
- The timing of this course was appropriate for me.

Open-Ended Questions

- What information from this course has been most relevant to our job?
- Was there any information that should be added to this course to make it more relevant to your work?

Customer Satisfaction

Rating Scale Questions

- I would recommend this course to others with jobs similar to mine.
- Taking this course was a good use of my time.

Open-Ended Questions

- Looking back, how could this program have been improved?
- Looking back, what would you change about this course?

Delayed Level 2: Learning

Knowlege/Skill

If it is important for your chain of evidence, you can re-measure knowledge or skill. These questions will be specific to the content taught.

Open-Ended Questions

- Looking back, what content do you remember most?
- Looking back, what content do you wish was covered that wasn't?

Attitude

Rating Scale Questions

- It is clear why it was important for me to attend this training.

Open-Ended Questions

- In your own words, explain why it was important for you to attend this course.

Level 3: Behavior

On-the-Job Behavior

Rating Scale Questions

- I have been successful in applying what I learned in training back on the job.
- I have been able to apply what I learned in class on the job.
- **Instructions:** Using this rating scale, circle the rating that best describes your current level of on-the-job application of each listed behavior.

Scale

1	2	3	4	5
Little or no application	Mild degree of application	Moderate degree of application	Strong degree of application	Very strong degree of application, and desire to help others do the same

Insert behavioral objective #1	1	2	3	4	5
Insert behavioral objective #2	1	2	3	4	5
Insert behavioral objective #3	1	2	3	4	5
Insert behavioral objective #4	1	2	3	4	5
Insert behavioral objective #5	1	2	3	4	5

- Please select the statement that best reflects your experience:

_____ I was able to apply what I learned within a week.

_____ I was able to apply what I learned within 2–4 weeks.

_____ I was able to apply what I learned 1–3 months after taking the class.

_____ I was not able to apply what I learned but plan to in the future.

_____ I was not able to apply what I learned and do not expect to apply it at any time in the future.

Other (please explain): _____

Open-Ended Questions

- Describe your experience in attempting to apply what you learned in training back on the job.
- To what degree have you applied what you learn.
- Have you struggled with application? If so, to what do you attribute your difficulty?
- What steps do you plan to take in the future to continue your progress?

Drivers

Rating Scale Questions

- My supervisor and I set expectations for this training before class.
- My supervisor and I determined how I would apply what I learned after training.
- I have recieved performance support in order to apply what I have learned successfully.
- I recieved support and encouragement for applying my learning to my job.
- I have the necessary resources to apply what I learned to my job.
- A system of accountability exists that helps me apply what I learned.

- Incentives exist to encourage me to apply what I learned.
- When I apply what I learned, I am rewarded appropriately.

Open-Ended Questions

- What additional training or support do you need to increase your effectiveness?
- What kind of support have you recieved that has helped you to implement what you learned?

Level 4: Results

Learning Indicators

Rating Scale Questions

- I am already seeing positive results from the training.
- I am expecting positive results from this initiative in the future.

Open-Ended Questions

- What early indicators of positive impact have you noticed from your efforts? How do you feel about those successes?

Targeted Results

- My successful outcomes are a result of the following factors (check all that apply):

____ Formal training	____ On-the-job learning
____ Coaching from a supervisor	____ Support from peers
____ Good mentoring	____ Good role modeling
____ A good system of accoutability	____ Positive recognition
____ Proper rewards and incentives	____ My own self determination

Open-Ended Questions

- To what degree have the results you expected actually occured?
- What additional outcomes are you hoping to achieve from your efforts?

🅐 Fuel Up: Chapter Exercise: High-Impact Evaluation

Now, it's your turn. What are the high-impact evaluation points for your organization and training program? Answer the questions below.

1. Who are your stakeholders? To whom will you be presenting your findings? In what format? Are they interested in qualitative or quantitative data?

2. What kinds of information will your stakeholders want to see to ensure the effectiveness of your training program on company goals? (level 4)

3. What kinds of measurements will show that behavior has changed on the job? (level 3)

4. What can you measure during the training event to show that learning has occurred? (level 2)

5. What story are you going to tell? (level 1)

Fuel Up: Chapter Tool: Evaluation Planning Worksheet

Evaluation is about more than throwing a survey at your learners. Use this worksheet to plan your evaluation process. For each of the evaluation factors listed, determine which are applicable to your project and which tools (surveys, interviews, tests, and so forth) you will use to measure each one. Remember multiple tools can be used for the same level.

What Will We Measure: (Evaluation Points)	How We Will Measure It: (Tools to Be Used)	When We Will Measure It: (Timing of Evaluation Method)
Level 1: Expectations • Relevance • Satisfaction		
Level 2: Learning • Objective 1 • Objective 2 • Objective 3		
Level 3: Behavior • Job Skill 1 • Job Skill 2 • Job Skill 3		
Level 4: Results • Business Goal 1 • Business Goal 2 • Business Goal 3		

MAINTENANCE

What's dangerous is not to evolve.

- Jeff Bezos

ROAD MAP: What to Expect

Fuel Up: Maintenance Tools and Templates

Tour Guide: Maintenance Case Study

Understanding When to Make Changes
by Jean Barbazette, Founder of The Training Clinic

Scenic Route: Quality Constraints on Maintenance

Business Alignment

By the Book: Basic Definitions and Information About Maintenance

Toll Lanes: Cost Constraints on Maintenance

Course Corrections and Save for the Future

Speed Limits: Time Constraints on Maintenance

Updating on the Fly and Creating an Archive

Maintenance: The Journey Home

After a great vacation, traveling back home can be bittersweet. By the time the engine has started and you hit the highway, you may already be thinking about your to-do list and the mounting email inbox waiting for you. It doesn't take long for the pressures of real life to overtake the residual feelings of your trip.

One underserved area of the training world is the ongoing maintenance of existing classes and events. It is very easy to let go of a class once it has been implemented—after all, if you did everything correctly, it should keep churning out value, right? You have new projects that need your attention, and you don't have the time or budget to spare on something already under way.

Over and over again, learning and development (L&D) professionals create a great training class, only to let it atrophy from neglect. Processes and attention are needed to keep training content relevant to the business and impactful for the audience.

In this chapter we discuss some of the methodologies for maintaining a successful training project, as well as how to finish out an offering in the most effective manner.

📖 By the Book: Maintenance

There just isn't a whole lot out there about maintaining and ending training programs! The hope is that you design once for a sustainable, valuable learning experience that lasts for quite a while. While that isn't always possible, there are plenty of ways to extend the shelf life of a training program—and, by doing so, to save yourself time and money—and provide outstanding quality!

Key Considerations:

- Continue level 1 and 2 evaluations (at least) to keep a pulse on the progress of the class.
- Schedule regular "check-ups" for ongoing training programs.
- When a training class ends, make sure to store digital files and content in an accessible place for use in other projects.
- Hold "lessons learned" sessions to inform future work.

The idea behind maintaining training classes is to keep them from getting stale by regularly checking in on key aspects of the content, and to keep it aligned with the organization.

When closing out a training program, make sure that you are able to leverage those resources in the future, rather than reinventing the wheel.

⏱ Speed Limits: Time Constraints

In a typical "update on the go" type of project, managing your time is going to be about quick efforts that return big impact. The risk point with training in maintenance mode, or ending, is that these projects tend to be a lower priority than new projects just starting up. However, investing a small amount of time, if effectively used, can have large returns.

1. Updating on the Fly—For ongoing training, there is a real risk of content becoming stagnant from neglect. This section discusses how to allot a short time to updates.

   a. Content and Materials Checklist

   b. Observer Double Duty

2. Archive—For training events that will be closed out, these ideas will help you store your resources for use at a later time.

   a. Creating an Archive

Updating on the Fly—Content and Materials Checklist

It's a good idea to keep tabs on class content and materials for needed updates. In general, using this checklist and making edits twice a year can help keep a training program on track—and save you time in the long run.

MATERIALS

1. Proper Names—Check people, places, company names, jargon, and abbreviations for changes and updates.

2. Technology—Look at software and hardware references to make sure everything is still relevant.

3. Screenshots—Software interfaces and websites change at an astonishing rate, so keep any screenshots you have updated.

4. Numbers—If you show statistics (for example, percent growth over the last five years) or numbers (for example, 650 people hired this year), keep them fresh. Also, check for dates.

5. Graphics and Images—Review graphics for relevance and trendiness.

CONTENT

6. Examples—Check to make sure the examples you use are still going to hit home for your learners.

7. Initiatives and Goals—This one is a little more subtle. Search content for references to organizational goals and initiatives and make sure that they are still going strong. For example, you might have referenced an initiative of "Hire! Retain! Promote!" but the language might have changed to "Building Leadership: Talent Management Program."

8. Alignment—I can't say this enough. Always ensure that your learning objectives are aligned with the goals of the organization!

Updating on the Fly—Observer Double Duty

Neglecting an ongoing course could take a toll in many ways. First, as we've discussed, the content could grow stagnant. Also, your stakeholders could start to question the value of a class that has been around for a while. Get your stakeholders involved in your class upkeep to address both issues at once.

First:

Set the Stage

1. Make any obvious changes or updates before involving stakeholders. They are not there to proofread your participant guides!

2. Set a meeting with the stakeholders you want to invite, individually, and explain that you are looking to get their input on making the training class more valuable.

3. Provide them with the questions that you would like answered. Allowing people to review and observe the class without any guidance is opening the floodgates to a host of criticism and unhelpful opinions.

Second:

The Questions

1. Essentially, the best thing to do is reframe your level 1 evaluation questions to be stakeholder-friendly. Here are some examples:

   a. If this was your first time observing the class, did the class meet your expectations? Why or why not?

   b. Did (fill in the blank with an activity) help clarify the roles on the financial team?

2. Ask direct questions about improving the class.

   a. How can we improve the class to be more in line with your vision for the organization?

1. Meet with each stakeholder-observer within a week of the event to get his or her feedback.

2. During the meeting, accept the feedback graciously and without taking it personally. Being defensive will not only lose you credibility points; it will also alienate the people you need behind the class. Depending on the advice, you may not want to implement every step suggested. Thank your stakeholders for their advice in any case, and don't make any decisions right away.

Third:

Debrief and

Follow-Through

3. Put small changes into action immediately, and make a plan for larger adjustments— then make sure you communicate this to the stakeholders to let them know you heard them and are taking action. If you decide not to put a suggestion into play right away, communicate that as well. Just make sure your decision is what's best for the learner and organization, and that you aren't just being stubborn!

Archive—Creating an Archive

Just as creating templates is crucial, keeping and storing digital files is very important to decreasing workload down the line. There are many archiving systems out there to choose from. If you can, utilize a system that specifically warehouses files, such as Microsoft's SharePoint. If you need to go with a more manual method, check out "How to Store It."

What to Store:

All files that may be needed in the future. Keep analysis tools and results, project plans, design documents, developed materials, handouts, and resources used during implementation, and everything associated with evaluation including tools, results, and all deliverables. If you keep more than the final version of files, clearly mark drafts in the file name. Make all file names descriptive!

How to Store It:

In a manual file system, keep files organized by project. Within the project folder, you may want to keep final versions of deliverables, and then additional folders per stage (ADDIE). It is also acceptable to create another folder devoted entirely to files that can be used as templates for future projects. Just to be sure that files are useful and multipurpose. Too much clutter can make the entire folder unuseable.

When to Store It:

It is best to save files into your archive as soon as they have been finalized, or after completing each step of the process. If you are on a tight deadline, however, this can be a low priority. Instead, build a due date into your project plan to devote to archiving all files. Don't forget that being able to find this information later will save you a ton of development time!

How to Recall It:

There's no use in creating an archive if you aren't going to use it again. If your archive system allows for keyword searches, make sure to add all relevant keywords to your files when storing them. This should include the project name, ADDIE step, date, and key content phrases. Avoid using names or initials in an archive; they are usually irrelevant later when reusing files.

$ Toll Lanes: Cost Constraints

Unfortunately, classes that get ignored for long periods will get out of alignment with the organization, and then need complete costly overhauls. Instead, keep ongoing costs low by checking the pulse of your training program.

1. Course Corrections—Leverage your subject matter experts (SMEs) and resources to help with the burden of keeping classes fresh and updated.

    a. Updates by Committee

2. Save for the Future—Capture important milestones, achievements, and obstacles to improve future projects.

    a. Easy Lessons Learned

Course Corrections—Updates by Committee

If you have an ongoing long-term training program, there is a risk in letting it run without periodic review. Overall, training classes need some sort of update and check-in at least twice a year. The best way to get this done on a low budget is to invite some SMEs to help with the process. Here is a sample process that you can adapt for your own situation.

Observation by Invitation		
Committee members are invited to observe the training class if they have not done so in the last few months.	Members should be a small group of outstanding performers and a few key stakeholders.	Provide a copy of the training review checklist from the end of this chapter.

Setting the Stage		
Gather the group's feedback prior to meeting and compile data.	Schedule an appropriate amount of time to cover the entire training. A one-day worshop might need a three-hour review.	Keep the meeting structured. Set expectations with an agenda and follow it.

The Framework for the Discussion	
Start with "mission critical" information—is the training class in alignment with the organization's goals? Does the learning from the class support the performance you want to see on the job?	Only after the group has come to an agreement on the strategic topics should you move on to comments about individual activities and teaching methods.

Save for the Future—Easy Lessons Learned

If you are closing out a training program, it is a great idea to conduct a "lessons learned" meeting. This can be helpful for projects that went really well, really poorly, or anywhere in between. Why? Well, in this way, you can avoid costly mistakes in the future by preparing ahead of time!

Work with everyone involved from analysis to evaluation to gather feedback on the process and work on the training project. Depending on the size of the group, you may want to conduct several small meetings, or even interviews. Combine feedback into one document that is searchable and viewable by anyone on the team. It's also a great idea to keep an overall master "lessons learned" document for reference. This can help get future projects and new team members up to speed quicker and without repeating mistakes.

Here are some topics that you will want to cover in your meetings, and document for future projects. Make sure to keep the criticism focused on process, project, and content—and not on an individual. Performance of a team member should be handled through proper channels.

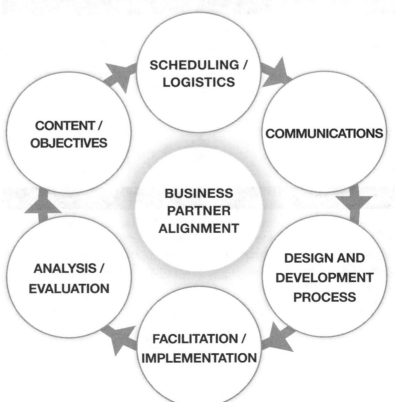

⬟ Scenic Route: Quality or Scope Constraints

Don't assume that if you aren't hearing complaints about the training class, everything is perfect. Be vigilant while maintaining training projects that the value being added is as high as it can be.

1. Business Alignment—Make sure that you periodically calibrate the class to ensure it is still adding value.

   a. Re-analyze and Re-evaluate

   b. Linking Training Programs

Business Alignment—Re-analyze and Re-evaluate

The primary need for an ongoing training class is the need to continuously align the direction of the class with the organization's goals and vision. This doesn't mean that you need to start over every time an email comes out from your CEO or client. If you keep the business at the core of everything you do, you won't have any problem.

Re-Analyze

Business Results Analysis:

Check in with your stakeholders very regularly to align with the business. See Business Case on page 26 for more!

Behavior Change:

Revisit the job task analysis every year or so. Jobs change because of policy, technology, change in leadership, and other factors.

Learning Goals:

Make sure that your learning objectives still support the desired behavior change. If the performance changes, the learning has to also!

Audience Analysis:

Keep trending data to see changes in important learner characteristics. Be sure to keep an eye out for potential ways to increase the WIIFM for the learner.

Re-Evaluate

Level 1 Evaluation:

Adjust your level 1s to keep up with changes in learner population and expectations of the class.

Level 2 Evaluation:

Make sure your level 2 learning evaluations are always in sync with changes to your objectives and learning activities.

Level 3 Evaluation:

Continue to monitor behavior change after your training event. Whether this is a new training or ongoing, the true value of a class is in its ability to increase performance.

Level 4 Evaluation:

When you check in with your stakeholders for alignment, ask about results metrics as well. Remember to measure what matters to them!

Business Alignment—Linking Training Programs

In an ideal world, we don't create "events"—one-time learning situations that stand alone. We want to create learning processes— ongoing development with consistent language and a consistent message that is high-touch and effective.

Most L&D professionals find it difficult to create a learning process when they are focused on getting a new class up and running on tight deadlines and budgets. Instead, it is beneficial to take a second look at the program after it has been implemented to "turn it up a notch" and make a bigger impact. These are all small changes you can make to increase the value of long-term training programs.

Link All Training Programs				
Use consistent language for goals, tasks, skills, competencies, and content.	If you use communication or process models in one class, reference as necessary in other classes.	Leverage tools (especially evaluation tools) across multiple training programs to save time and for consistency.	Create branding or specific visual styles for a series of related training programs to increase the perception of value.	Link all training programs to competencies, and track employees on individual development plans.

The more you chain training programs together, the more you create ongoing learning and development. Ultimately, a stand-alone training is faulty in that we, as adult learners, usually need follow-up and support to make a permanent behavior change. Creating cohesive, ongoing, and linked training programs will help create the results that you want to see.

👤 Tour Guide: Case Study: Understanding When to Make Changes

Jean Barbazette, Founder, The Training Clinic
email: Info@thetrainingclinic.com or visit www.thetrainingclinic.com.

There are at least six types of course maintenance for the course designer to consider:

1. Preventive maintenance

2. New version or enhancement of software, policy, or procedure

3. A change imposed by a regulation or corporate requirement

4. Change in performance by employees

5. A discretionary change by the course designer

6. A need has been fulfilled

Preventive Maintenance

Courses can have a regularly scheduled timeframe to identify updates from learners or the field that suggest changes to the course are needed. A new example might provide a better learning experience or improve retention.

New Version or Enhancement

As equipment or software versions and improvements occur, courses need to be updated. A process or procedure may have been refined, and courses need to be updated accordingly.

Imposed Changes

Corporate requirements and government regulations affect many processes and procedures. To bring training programs into compliance, updates are needed.

Performance Issue

If the target population is younger, older, or more diverse than when the course was designed, then updates are needed. Perhaps performance changes, such as an increase in the accident or incident rate, would call for an update of the course. If the organization has gone through a merger, then course content might need to change prior to a rollout for the new population.

Discretionary Change

Occasionally, course designers might make a formatting change or a change in the appearance of course materials. If a classroom training session is converted to an online session, perhaps the format of the course materials might need to be changed to accommodate the new medium. These types of changes ought to be related to bottom-line results to avoid incurring unnecessary costs.

Saturated Market

Finally, when a training need has been fulfilled, it is appropriate to discontinue a course that is no longer needed.

The following chart blends these six types of course maintenance into the ADDIE model of course design.

Type of Maintenance	Assess	Design
1. Preventive	Identify frequency required	Identify utility of content
2. New version	Match the upgrade to task and to population	Map to previous version
3. Legal or headquarters requirement	Task analysis	New module
4. Performance: e.g., accident rate increases	Performance analysis	Create design if skill deficiency
5. Performance: e.g., target population changes	Target population	Identify content to revise
6. Discretionary	Assess cost of current use versus cost to develop enhancements	Identify enhancements
7. Saturated market	Current use versus cost	Convert to online archive

Develop	Implement	Evaluate
Write new examples	Try out and practice	Test or skill observation
Write new examples	Try out and practice	Test or skill observation
New activity	Try out	Test or skill observation Level 4 results
Create practice exercises	Amount of practice	Skill test or observation
New examples	Amount of practice	Test or skill observation
Convert materials	Replace older materials	Reaction of learners
Write support materials	Synchronous training	Test or skill observation

🅑 Fuel Up: Chapter Exercise: Create an Easy Digital Archive

1. What is your purpose for creating an archive? (Free up hard drive space? Make documents available to teammates? Create a searchable database of resources?)

2. Where will you store your files to meet your purpose in question 1?

3. Will you store files after the completion of a project or intermittently throughout the project? If backing up during a project, determine the schedule for storing files.

4. List the files you will store for each of the project steps. Consider word processor documents, spreadsheets, databases, images, graphics, and other working files.

    Analysis (Plans, Tools, Results):

    Design (Storymaps, Outlines):

    Develop (Workbooks, Job Aids, Handouts, Presentations, Modules):

    Implement (Logistics, Facilitator Preparation):

    Evaluate (Plans, Tools, Results):

5. Determine file naming conventions for all files.

6. Who will have access to the files?

7. Decide on a timeframe for revisiting project files in the future. After all, storing files indefinitely only helps if someone remembers that they are there!

🅟 Fuel Up: Training Program Review Checklist

	Proper Names: People, places, company names, jargon, and abbreviations
	Technology: Software and hardware
	Screenshots
	Numbers: Statistics, trending data, historical data, dates
	Graphics and Images
	Examples
	Initiatives and Goals
	Alignment: Objectives are aligned with the goals of the organization

SUMMARY

The real voyage of discovery consists not in
seeking new landscapes but in having new eyes.

- Marcel Proust

The Journey So Far

The trip is over, your budget is spent, and your time is up. Hopefully, all of your hard work and preparation delivered a memorable journey. At the beginning, you focused on answering key questions about your destination and the trip you wanted to take, then you figured out what exactly your vacation would look like, and you made your reservations. While you were away, you took photos and enjoyed yourself, and then came back and shared stories and pictures with friends. With careful planning, you may have even seen everything you wanted to see and stayed within your vacation budget.

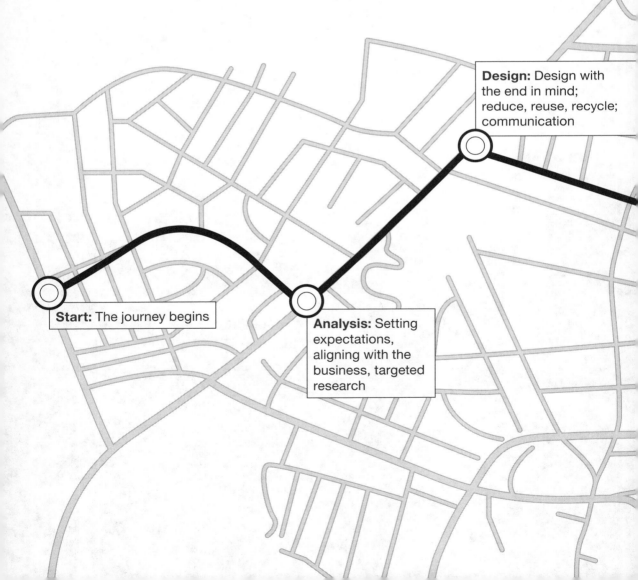

Design: Design with the end in mind; reduce, reuse, recycle; communication

Start: The journey begins

Analysis: Setting expectations, aligning with the business, targeted research

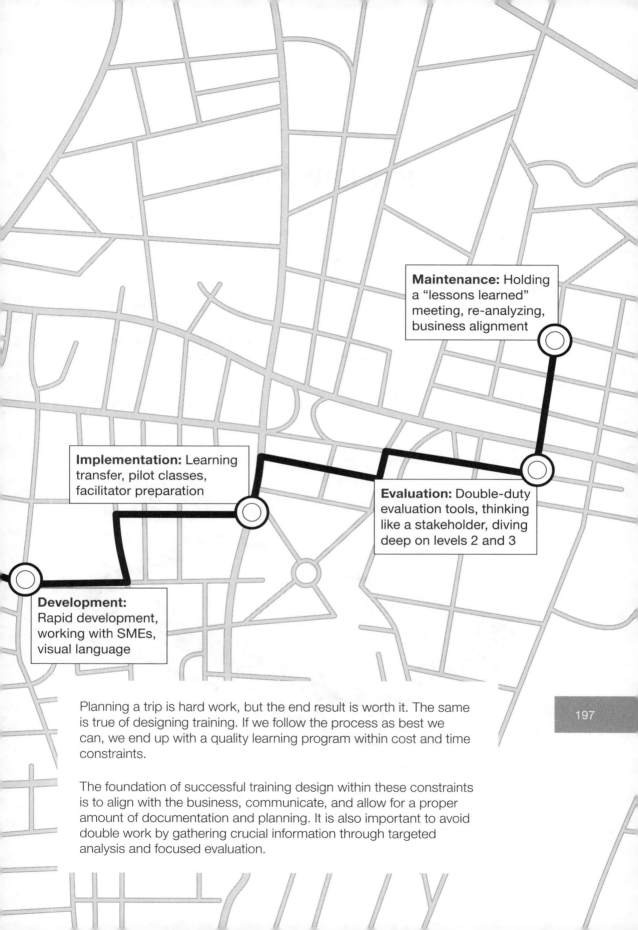

Maintenance: Holding a "lessons learned" meeting, re-analyzing, business alignment

Implementation: Learning transfer, pilot classes, facilitator preparation

Evaluation: Double-duty evaluation tools, thinking like a stakeholder, diving deep on levels 2 and 3

Development: Rapid development, working with SMEs, visual language

Planning a trip is hard work, but the end result is worth it. The same is true of designing training. If we follow the process as best we can, we end up with a quality learning program within cost and time constraints.

The foundation of successful training design within these constraints is to align with the business, communicate, and allow for a proper amount of documentation and planning. It is also important to avoid double work by gathering crucial information through targeted analysis and focused evaluation.

Bringing It All Home

This book has addressed a lot of best practices and methods for coping with real-world constraints on training projects. We have covered everything from dealing with stakeholders and subject matter experts (SMEs) to targeting analysis and evaluation.

The path of an instructional designer is never a smooth one, with leisurely amounts of time and ample budgets—but it can still be enjoyable. Learn the common potholes to avoid, and pack your suitcase with plenty of templates, skills, and constant communication. With the proper effort and preparation, you will be able to navigate like a pro.

Now, it's your turn to figure out what your next training road trip will look like. I wish you an exciting and rewarding journey!

"It is good to have an end to journey toward; but it is the journey that matters in the end." – Ursula K. LeGuin

Appendixes:

Appendix A: Website Information

Please visit **www.terpassociates.com** for:

- updates to content within this book
- opportunities to discuss book topics with other "real-world" designers
- links to the best L&D sites on the web
- opportunities to share your best practices and lessons learned
- news from around the industry.

And…more tools, tips, tricks, and best practices for beating your constraints!

Appendix B: Resource List

If you:

…want to know how to get your message across, tell a story, or build excitement with your presentations:

Duarte Design: **http://www.duarte.com/**

…want to work with a world-class organizational development consultant with a library of published books and extensive expertise:

ebb associates: **http://www.ebbweb.com/**

…want to learn more about training design, instructional systems design, or the ADDIE model:

ASTD: **http://www.astd.org/**

…want to know even more about project management for trainers:

Russell Martin & Associates: **http://www.russellmartin.com/**

…want to talk to some top-notch change experts, who have a ton of experience in the L&D industry:

Emerson Human Capital Consulting: **http://emersonhc.com/**

...want to learn how to move ideas into action, through exercising influence and innovation management:

Barnes & Conti: **http://www.barnesconti.com/**

…want to dive deeper into informal learning and how it has changed the way we think about learning:

C4LPT: **http://c4lpt.co.uk/**

...want to hear from the innovators of informal learning:

Internet Time Alliance: **http://internettimealliance.com/wp/**

…want to know how to ENGAGE your audience, through brilliant design:

Ken Blanchard Companies: **http://www.kenblanchard.com/ brilliancebydesign/**

…want to improve your facilitation delivery from the leader in train-the-trainer certifications:

The Training Clinic: **http://www.thetrainingclinic.com/**

…want to get a sense of real-world evaluations and how to measure what matters:

Kirkpatrick Partners: **http://www.kirkpatrickpartners.com**

Appendix C: List of Chapter Exercises and Tools

	Exercises	**Tools**
Analysis	Aligning Project Goals With Business Goals	Short but Sweet Survey
Design	Design Map	Storymap
Development	Course Look and Feel	Materials Review Checklist
Implementation	Follow-Up Activity	Facilitator Preparation Checklist
Evaluation	High-Impact Evaluation	Evaluation Planning Worksheet
Maintenance	Creating an Easy Digital Archive	Training Program Review Checklist

Index

About the Author

For 10 years, Jenn Labin has worked with organizations to improve workforce performance through leadership development and summits, formal and informal training, change efforts, and employee engagement programs. Jenn has contributed articles to the Pfeiffer Annuals in Consulting and Training. Credentials include an MA in Instructional Systems Design, and certifications in DISC-PIAV, Kirkpartick Four levels, Leadership Program Development, and Presentation Design. Besides training, Jenn is passionate about scuba diving, the environment, and spending time with family. Jenn lives near Baltimore, MD with her amazing husband, daughter, and two turtles.

T.E.R.P. associates, LLC
Training | Engagement | Retention | Performance